RARE Cases

Book #1

*In The New Testament with <u>Possibilities of Interpretation</u>; on Passages of Intrigue and Enigma **in the 4 Gospels**.*

By José E. Espinoza

SERIES: "RARE Cases in the New Testament of The Bible with Possibilities of Interpretation; on Passages of Intrigue and Enigma"

José E. Espinoza

Note from the Author:

To my dear readers, and with all due respect to the other writers, scholars, theologians and interpreters of any portion if the Holy Scriptures (The Bible); Unless it literally says ("*written") in a complete sentence, paragraph or statement, such as *<u>Genesis 1:1</u> *"*<u>*In the beginning God created the heavens and earth</u>." (That is what is *written, that is what it *means. And therefore, *<u>it does not need any additional interpretation</u>). Otherwise, no matter who say it or write about it, either <u>as a commentary</u>, <u>personal point of view</u>, or a <u>theological explanation</u>, it is simply a **POSSIBILITY OF INTERPRETATION**, nothing more and/or nothing less.

– José E. Espinoza

RARE CASES Book #1

Dedication

To a <u>Human Being Interested</u> in the Biblical Records of the Holy Scriptures, with the Desire and Purpose <u>to Know and Understand</u> the <u>Secrets of the Kingdom </u>of God.

- José E. Espinoza

RARE CASES Book #1

This Book Belong to:

_____

José E. Espinoza

Table of Contents

Introduction

Have you ever wondered why certain stories in the Gospels feel so unusual, **RARE,** or enigmatic, almost as if these **CASES** don't quite fit with the predictable flow of miracles and parables? Maybe it is a detail that surprises you in these **INTRIGUING** passages of the New Testament such as—a **baby leaping** in the mother's womb 'empowered' by The Holy Spirit, a star that 'moves and stops', a **prophet** 'living on locusts and honey', or **an angel** who 'quietly appears in someone's dream'. These moments are easy to overlook, but for anyone curious enough to slow down and really look on to these cases, **they open doors to deeper questions** about faith, purpose, and the very nature of God's work in the world.

This book is designed for those who want to go beyond surface readings—especially young Christians and new believers searching for real substance in their faith journey, Bible study leaders hoping to spark new conversations, and readers who crave honest explanations for some of the Gospel's most puzzling moments. Here, we pause over the rare cases scattered throughout the four Gospels, treating each one not as a footnote, but as <u>an invitation to explore the extraordinary</u> ways that God acts, speaks, and reveals himself. **These passages** may seem **<u>enigmatic</u>** at first, but within them lie keys to understanding God's character—and our own walk with Him—in ways we might never have imagined.

What makes these stories or rare cases stand out? For starters, they challenge assumptions. We expect callings to come to adult faith stages after years of developing wisdom, yet the story of John the Baptist throws this notion into question as he is filled with the Holy Spirit before birth. How do we make sense of Mary's impossible pregnancy or Joseph's life-altering guidance through dreams? Why would the Gospels devote such attention to a moving star, wild beasts in the desert, or the brief visit of angels, and yet leave years of Jesus' adolescence summarized in a single verse? These questions aren't just trivia for Bible experts—they're touch points for anyone seeking to understand how faith interacts with real life, uncertainty, and even apparent contradiction.

<u>Many books</u> provide a straightforward retelling of the life of Jesus, his teachings, his sacrifice, and his resurrection. **But far fewer linger over the <u>rare</u> details—the outliers that defy easy explanation.** Yet those are often the places where we find ourselves most challenged in our reading, whether alone, in small groups, or classroom settings. **This book aims** to turn those moments of confusion or curiosity into

a source of growth and discussion rather than frustration or doubt. Each chapter takes up one of these rare cases, drawing from careful analysis and accessible insights, always with the goal of making complex ideas understandable and deeply relevant for today.

As you read, you'll discover that **the New Testament is rich with mystery and meaning** beneath its familiar surface. The stories explored here cut across boundaries of culture, time, and tradition; they refuse to be compacted into tidy formulas or shallow morals. Instead, they prompt reflection on what it truly means to encounter God—not just in what's easily explained, but in those experiences that stretch our understanding and prompt us to ask bigger questions.

Consider the way the Gospels introduce major players not with grand fanfare, but through quiet, sometimes bewildering acts: a newborn recognized as king by foreign sages following an unpredictable star, a boy in the temple astonishing learned teachers at age twelve, a preacher emerging from the wilderness in strange clothes, heralding a turning point for the world. Each episode calls us to rethink our definitions of calling, greatness, and spiritual readiness. Why highlight these oddities? Because the Gospels seem intent on showing that God's ways are rarely bound by human limitations, timelines, or cultural expectations.

For study group leaders and educators, **these passages can become valuable teaching moments**. They push us to wrestle with ambiguity, appreciate multiple valid interpretations, and accept that sometimes faith means living in the tension between mystery and revelation. The explanations offered here avoid technical language and heavy academic argumentation. Instead, the focus is on clarity, approachable reasoning, and room for honest exploration—qualities that foster genuine engagement among youth and seekers alike.

At every step, you'll find encouragement to think critically, reflect prayerfully, and discuss openly. Scripture itself models this approach: the early church debated, questioned, and interpreted together, learning that vibrant faith isn't threatened by tough passages but is actually enriched by them. By examining miracle stories alongside genealogies, visions, rituals, and more, we develop a toolkit for handling not only "textbook" belief, but also real-life situations full of doubt, change, and discovery.

A central conviction behind this collection is that God works just as powerfully in hidden or confusing moments as in dramatic interventions. Whether it's **Simeon** waiting faithfully **to see the Messiah** before dying, Jesus stepping forward for baptism though without need for repentance, or the Spirit leading him deliberately into temptation, these scenes remind us that divine purpose often unfolds long before we recognize it. **Sometimes the most important lessons** come not from what is shouted loudly, but whispered quietly. In fact, the very "silences" in the Gospels (like **Jesus' silent growing-up** years) carry as much weight as the wonders and words. They teach humility, patience, and the value of steady, unseen preparation.

Most importantly, approaching these rare cases can deepen your confidence that **faith does not depend on having all the answers**. It's possible, and even necessary, to live with questions and trust that God welcomes your curiosity—even your doubts—as part of your spiritual development. As you travel through chapters focused on challenging passages, you'll see practical ways to engage with difficult verses: reading closely for context, seeking the bigger picture, praying for insight, and leaning on the wisdom of trusted community. You'll also find tools for discerning when a passage may be misapplied or twisted, protecting yourself and others from confusion or deception by building habits of critical thinking, spiritual openness, and mutual accountability.

Throughout the book, you're reminded again and again: **God's Word** is not just something to be dissected or mastered, but something to be lived and experienced. The same Spirit who inspired these rare moments in history is present now, guiding you toward greater maturity, resilience, and hope—whether you're approaching the Bible for the first time or leading others toward deeper truth. Each rare case offers a jumping-off point for ongoing conversation, inspiring you to look for God's presence not just in the spectacular, but in the overlooked and ordinary events of daily life.

Whether you are searching for answers to longstanding questions, preparing for a youth group lesson, or simply eager to move beyond familiar verses, **this book provides a guide for digging deeper**. You'll emerge better equipped to face uncertainty, more comfortable with complexity, and more appreciative of the layered richness that makes the Gospels endlessly fascinating. **These rare cases** won't just fill your mind with theological facts; they will shape how you approach Scripture, yourself, and others—with curiosity, humility, and expectancy for God's surprising grace.

So, as you begin this exploration, bring your whole self—questions, hopes, hesitations, and all. Expect to have your perspective stretched and your understanding deepened. Let these uncommon stories challenge the boundaries of what you thought possible, and may you find, in the pages ahead, both the courage to engage mysterious truths and the joy of discovering that faith thrives best when it makes space for wonder, dialogue, and growth.

Part 1:

RARITY In ...

A 'NEW ERA'

Chapter 1:

Rare Case of …

A BABY

Filled with the Holy Spirit Before Being Born

Luke 1:15, & Luke 1:41 (Bible) – New Living Translation

In The New Testament with Possibilities of Interpretation;

Uniqueness of A Rare Prophet: John the Baptist "Filled with the Holy Spirit" Still in the Mother's Womb

What it means (in this case) to be chosen for a 'special purpose' even before you take your first breath? Can someone be set apart or **filled with power of the Holy Spirit while still in the womb**? These ideas might seem strange or even impossible, especially when we consider how most people begin their journeys—growing, learning, and discovering their roles through experience. But what if there was a story that challenges this common understanding? What if one person's life was marked by divine purpose from the very start, shaping everything they would become? To be filled with the Holy Spirit before birth? How could **a child still in the womb** carry such a powerful sign of God's presence and purpose? What does this early anointing tell us about **John the Baptist** and hid unique role in the history of salvation? These questions invite us to explore an extraordinary detail found in one of the most unexpected places in the scriptures of the New Testament. By examining the ancient world's understanding of the Holy Spirit, the rich symbolism behind prenatal calling, and the way this idea challenges common assumptions, we open a window into how God's plans and unfold even before life begins. And at the same time, such questions invite us to think deeply about calling, destiny, and the ways something greater might be at work, quietly and powerfully, long before we notice. This chapter asks us to explore those mysteries and to reflect on what it truly means to be set apart from the beginning. Also, it will guide us through fresh perspective that deepen our grasp of John's identity and the meaning behind Luke's remarkable claim, offering insights that will inspire thoughtful reflection and lively discussion.

Historical and Theological Context of John's Prenatal Inspiration

John the Baptist's story opens with a detail that can surprise anyone reading Luke's Gospel with fresh eyes. **Luke 1:15** says **John** *"will be filled with the Holy Spirit, even **before** he is **born**,"* a statement that raises bold questions about how God chooses and empowers His servants. In the ancient world, and in Jewish tradition, the idea of someone receiving the Spirit before birth would have seemed almost unthinkable. **The Holy Spirit**, or Ruach HaKodesh, was understood as the powerful, personal presence of God, the One who inspired prophets, revealed God's words, and stirred hearts to action. Moses, Samuel, Elijah, and others acted under the Spirit's influence, but their empowerment always had a beginning point—often as adults or during a key event. In most cases, this divine filling lasted only during their prophetic work or a particular season of their calling. John's experience, as presented in Luke, stands out in vivid contrast.

To grasp why this detail is extraordinary, it helps to understand the context in which Luke's audience heard these words. In the Hebrew Scriptures, the Spirit came upon certain people at specific times. Samson received strength from the Spirit at moments of crisis; Saul, while still a shepherd, was transformed into "another man" only once God chose him for kingship (1 Samuel 10:6). The pattern repeated: the Spirit came and went, marking divine approval for a task or prophecy. Even strong figures like Jeremiah, who God knew before he was formed in the womb (Jeremiah 1:5), did not have Scripture say the Spirit filled them from before birth.

Luke singles out John in a way that breaks this pattern. Luke claims **John** (Later called "John the Baptist") *"will be filled with the Holy Spirit, even before he is born"*—not just touched with the Spirit for a moment or a mission, but shaped and marked by a divine power from the beginning. This marked difference would have caught the attention of any Jewish reader who reflected on the ways God moved in the past. John's filling is not described as an ordinary gift; it is an extraordinary calling, a sign that foretells a life lived as God's instrument.

Connecting to the wider biblical tradition, almost every great prophet received their calling through a vision, a voice, or a dramatic event as adults or young people. Only a handful of stories bear any hint of God's selection from before birth. The stories of Samson (Judges 13) and, in a different sense, Jeremiah, come closest, but neither states outright that the Spirit dwelled in them as infants or unborn children.

With John, Luke insists that from his earliest existence, he would be a vessel of God's Spirit, already set apart.

What does this mean for John's identity and his impact on the story of salvation? In Jewish thought, the one marked by God from before birth would stand as a living sign of God's purposeful action. Instead of waiting for a moment of recognition or a crisis to show devotion, John begins life already empowered. This sets the tone for his destiny. He does not grow into his role by accident or even through personal striving. He is born into his mission, with every future step foreshadowed by this first miraculous anointing.

Luke's way of telling the story points to deeper truths about how God works. The detail is not just historical—it is theological. Luke sets up John as a revolutionary figure. **He is the last prophet before Jesus**, and <u>his Spirit-filled beginning announces a new chapter</u>. John's message—bold, convicting, fearless—flows from this deep well of Holy Spirit-given authority. His strict way of life, his total commitment to his task, and his willingness to confront power flow from that original filling.

John's story invites readers to contemplate the mystery of divine election and the possibilities of Spirit-led living. When considering this account, each person can reflect on how God's purposes sometimes unfold in ways far outside normal expectations. The idea that someone could be chosen and filled with the Holy Spirit, even before their birth opens up fresh questions about calling, readiness, and trust in God's bigger design. The story stands as an invitation to personal wonder and exploration of how God continues to shape lives with purpose.

José E. Espinoza

Interpretive Possibilities of John's Early Calling

Luke's account of John the Baptist's prenatal encounter with the Holy Spirit stands out in the Gospel's opening chapters and is expressed most clearly in **Luke 1:15** and **Luke 1:41**. These verses form the core textual platform for exploring how the early church, biblical interpreters, and modern readers have understood this extraordinary event. As the narrative unfolds, John is introduced not only as a prophet but as someone marked by the Spirit's presence even before birth, a detail Luke highlights twice. These signal moments have inspired a range of interpretations that each illuminate something different about John's identity and Luke's theological emphasis.

John's Spirit-filling before birth is a detail that continues to generate awe and curiosity. The idea stands out within ancient Jewish thought, where prophetic empowerment almost always belonged to adults marked by special callings. Old Testament stories tell of individuals like Samson and Samuel who received the Spirit for specific roles, yet none claim a prophetic endowment even before birth quite like John's. When Luke introduces this scene (Luke 1:15), the words shape John's entire identity in the minds of early readers: here is a prophet like no other, already set apart by God for a lifelong mission, his destiny unfolding before he ever drew breath. This surprising element frames the questions that arise—what does it actually mean to be filled with the Holy Spirit from the womb, and how do we speak of such an experience?

POSSIBILITY OF INTERPRETATION 1:

A literal, Supernatural <u>Filling</u> while <u>still in the womb</u>

A first way to read Luke's statement is in the most literal sense: John received a real, immediate endowment of the Holy Spirit while still in Elisabeth's womb. This reading leans heavily on moments like Luke 1:41, when John leaps in response to Mary's greeting. Some see in this leap a sign of spiritual awareness, as if the presence of Jesus—now carried by Mary—stirs something purposeful in the unborn John. This kind of filling suggests John already enjoyed a deep connection to God even before birth, an awareness that surpasses normal human development. He embodies the wonder of a life touched by God before any human achievement or even choice; the Holy Spirit initiated his prophetic journey right from the start. For those who hold this view, John's spiritual authority and mission are both miraculous and unique, presenting him as a living sign of God's power and intention to intervene in human history. According to – *Everett's Study Notes on the Holy Scriptures - Bible Commentaries Luke 1.(2025).* This literal understanding lines up with the Gospel's repeated mention of people being "filled" with the Spirit and acting in extraordinary ways, marking John as an exceptional vessel from the very beginning.

POSSIBILITY OF INTERPRETATION 2:

Symbolic filling indicating God's choice and protection

For others, Luke's words carry more of a symbolic or theological weight than a strictly literal one. In this perspective, being "filled with the Holy Spirit from the womb" signals God's special election, favor, and protection over John, without implying a physical possession by the Spirit before birth. The phrase becomes a way to describe God's sovereign and guiding hand in John's life, affirming John's role as a chosen servant and a vessel set apart by divine grace. Biblical language often works this way, using the language of fullness and blessing to sum up a person's relationship to God's plan (see stories of Jeremiah or Isaiah, marked as chosen from the womb yet not described as literally filled with the Spirit at that age). In John's case, the declaration matches the signs already woven through the birth narrative—his mother's miraculous pregnancy, the angelic pronouncements, and the wonder that surrounds his early childhood. **John life purpose,** his calling, and even his challenges unfold under God's watchful care, demonstrate a walking testimony of God's providence, a life shaped by God's will even before his ministry began in public.

POSSIBILITY OF INTERPRETATION 3:

A prenatal Sign of the Coming Messianic Era

There is also a view that John's prenatal Spirit-filling marks the <u>start of a new era in salvation history</u>. Here, John stands as a <u>bridge</u>; **he is the <u>last and greatest prophet</u>** of the old age and <u>the forerunner to something new</u>. Luke's careful attention to prophecy and fulfillment (noted throughout chapters 1–3) makes John's filling a signal of what God is about to do through Jesus. The Spirit's presence in John's earliest days becomes a preview of the wider outpouring that characterizes the coming Messianic age. This reading traces a dramatic shift—John's Spirit-empowerment is about more than his personal calling; it is about God bringing in a new chapter for Israel and the world. His function in life position him as the final point in the last sentence, opening a new paragraph for humanity.

POSSIBILTY OF INTERPRETATION 4:

Connection to Old Testament Prophetic Traditions

Some see in John's experience echoes of Old Testament stories. Samson was to be a Nazirite from birth, his strength and Spirit-empowerment promised before he was born. Samuel's mother dedicated him to God's service before his birth, and his entire childhood was spent in the temple's shadow. These parallels character's examples invite a sense of continuity, affirming that John's story is both new and deeply rooted in the rhythms of God's dealings with Israel and the rest of the world. John's filling with The Holy Spirit before birth offers inspiration to many. It suggests that divine calling, protection, and purpose may arrive long before any of us can claim our own achievements, challenging readers to wonder at the ways God works—sometimes quietly, unexpectedly, and always with meaning.

Each of these interpretations—supernatural literal filling, symbolic election, prophetic turning point, and Old Testament continuity—invite readers to consider John's prenatal calling with new depth and to reflect on the ways Luke's narrative reveals the mystery and intentionality of God's purposes at work even before life begins. Each angle adds fresh insight to John's prophetic identity and the shape of God's unfolding story.

Summary and Reflection of Chapter 1

Now that we have explored the rare and extraordinary detail of **John the Baptist being filled with the Holy Spirit before birth**, we can better appreciate how this rare event shapes his prophetic identity and Luke's larger message, helping our understanding of God's ways of calling and empowering people. This unique beginning invites us to see that <u>divine purpose often starts long before any visible action</u>, encouraging us to trust that God is at work in hidden and surprising ways. For young adults, Bible study leaders, and all who seek to grasp the depth of Scripture without confusion, John's story opens the door to rich conversations about faith, calling, and readiness. As we move forward, reflecting on John's prenatal anointing challenges us to consider how God might be shaping our own lives quietly and profoundly, inviting us to live with hope and openness to the Spirit's guidance from the very start.

Reference List of Chapter 1

Primary Biblical Reference:

Gospel of Luke 1:15, & **Luke 1:41**. Prediction about John the Baptist's; *being **"filled with The Holy Spirit, while in the mother's womb" and his future purpose and impact as a 'Prophet of the Highest"*** According to the Bible – New Living Translation

Other References:

Luke 1:15 - Verse-by-Verse Bible Commentary - StudyLight.org. (2025).

Luke 1 - Everett's Study Notes on the Holy Scriptures - Bible Commentaries - StudyLight.org. (2025).

Luke. (2025). - Soniclight.com

Chapter 2:

Rare Case of …

A PREGNANCY

The Most Enigmatic Conception

<u>Matthew 1:18</u> … "*while **she was still a virgin**, <u>she **became</u>
<u>pregnant**</u> through the power <u>**of the Holy Spirit**</u>.*" According to
(the Bible) – New Living Translation… & other versions…

José E. Espinoza

Unmatched Event in Human History

"How can this be, since I am a virgin?" Mary's question captures the wonder and confusion that has surrounded her pregnancy for centuries. In a world where conception always involved a man, the claim that she was pregnant through the Holy Spirit challenges everything people believed about life, family, and God's power. This story, preserved in the pages of the New Testament, is unlike any other—it invites us to pause and consider what it means for something truly new and unexpected to enter human history. As we explore this remarkable event, we will reflect on how it speaks to faith, tradition, and the ways people have understood the divine working in the ordinary moments of life.

Biblical and Historical Setting of Mary's Conception

*"This is how Jesus the Messiah was born. His mother, Mary, was engaged to be married to Joseph. But before the marriage took place, while she was still a **virgin**, she became **pregnant through** the power of the Holy Spirit"* – (**Matthew 1:18**, NLT). With this sentence, Matthew wastes no time establishing extraordinary circumstances.

The phrasing does more than launch the story. It rearranges the normal order readers might expect; engagement, consummation, then conception. Instead, something far from ordinary has taken place. Mary is pregnant before she lives together (having sexual intimacy) with Joseph, making it clear, from the start, that the birth of Jesus does not follow the well-known script for how ancestors, heirs, or everyday children came into being. The phrase **"with child of the Holy Spirit"** isn't just odd; it's unfamiliar in the world of first-century Jewish stories. According to *(Bible interpretation by Abraham Mutholath, 2024)* & (*Dr. Constable's Expository Notes, 2025)*. Here, Matthew prepares his audience to think about Jesus as both **<u>fully human</u>**—born to Mary—and **<u>fully divine—conceived</u>** <u>through the Holy Spirit</u>; God and man with us, or among us: 'Immanuel,' a name for God's own power and presence. This also can concord with to the scripture in **(Isaiah 7:14)** *"... the Lord himself will give you the sign. Look! The virgin will conceive a child! She will give birth to a son and will call him **<u>Immanuel</u>** (which means '**<u>God is with us</u>**')"*.

First-century Jews held definite ideas about what it meant for a woman to have a child, for herself, her family, and her community. Conception relied on sexual relations between a man and a woman; anything else was thought impossible and would be met with skepticism or outright disbelief. Medically, there was no concept of parthenogenesis or virgin conception. If a pregnancy occurred outside marriage or engagement, it could be seen as the result of adultery—sometimes a crime warranting severe punishment under Mosaic Law. Adultery brought shame, not just on the woman but also on her family, and could leave scars on a community's sense of honor. Virginity, especially for engaged women, carried enormous social weight. Family reputation often rested on a woman's purity before marriage, and public acknowledgment of sexual morality shaped an entire network of relationships. A claim that a young, engaged woman was with child, without having been with her husband, would be shocking and distressing, whether whispered among neighbors or declared in court. That's why Matthew's description would have been outrageous. Not only does it challenge biological understanding, but it also threatens the delicate fabric of Jewish community life, where boundaries and roles were watched closely and violations remembered for generations.

Engagement in that culture brought with it obligations <u>almost equal to marriage</u>. Joseph and Mary were recognized as legally bound, even without living together or having marital relations. If a woman became pregnant before her husband took her home, the community would assume infidelity. Joseph's situation becomes painfully clear. On learning of Mary's pregnancy, he risked public humiliation and probably faced the expectation to clear his own good name by charging Mary with wrongdoing. The Mosaic Law offered two main responses: make a public accusation, resulting in shame or even danger for Mary, or handle the matter privately. For Joseph, the news did not just disrupt plans for a family; it posed a deep challenge to honor, obedience, and compassion within strict boundaries. - (*MATTHEW 01:18-25: GOD'S INTERVENTION in the BIRTH of JESUS | Bible interpretation by Abraham Mutholath*, 2024; *Matthew*

1 - Dr. Constable's Expository Notes - Bible Commentaries - StudyLight.org). **Joseph's choice** to *"divorce her quietly"* reflects both the gravity of her social standing and his own righteous character; it prevents a public scandal, but also underscores how serious the accusation would have been.

Stories of God intervening in human reproduction stretch back through Hebrew Scriptures. Sarah's laughter at the idea of becoming pregnant in old age is recorded before Isaac's miraculous birth. Hannah prayed desperately in the temple, receiving Samuel after years of childlessness. Manoah's wife conceived Samson after an angelic promise. In each case, God acts where hope has faded, but always within the limits of sexual union that seemed impossible due to age or infertility. **Mary stands apart**. Her conception is not just surprising because of her youth or external barriers, but because it takes place without any male involvement at all. Only here does nature itself seem to bend outright, raising new questions about God's purposes for humanity. - (*MATTHEW 01:18-25: GOD'S INTERVENTION in the BIRTH of JESUS | Bible interpretation by Abraham Mutholath*,). The creative involvement of the Holy Spirit pushes the character of God as a life-giver into new territory—divine initiative beyond any precedent. The narrative invites readers to see continuity with an ancient God who disrupts natural processes, but also marks out this event as a first.

That such a claim would take shape in first-century Judea, a community steeped in tradition and watchful about transgression, sets the stage for debate. The virgin conception is not just a theological statement or an article of faith for later generations. It is, at its roots, a story that shocks, puzzles, and invites deep wonder. Many who encountered Matthew's Gospel would have found themselves faced with the same tension. The account of Mary's pregnancy collides with everyday expectations and throws wide the possibilities of how God's action in the world might be understood. The centuries since have only multiplied the questions and reflections sparked by this announcement, opening space for interpretations that try to make sense of both the claim and its consequences.

Interpretive Models of the Virgin Birth

First-century Jewish hopes for God's intervention set the scene for understanding the many ways people have approached the story of Mary's pregnancy with Jesus. Surrounded by expectations of prophetic fulfillment, the claims about Mary's conceiving a child while engaged to Joseph stand out as both spiritually charged and socially challenging. The Gospels of Matthew and Luke offer the main scriptural accounts, each building this event into a cornerstone for Christian faith and understanding.

PSSIBILITY OF INTERPRETATION 1:

The Virgin Birth as a **Literal Miracle**

Many Christians throughout history have embraced a literal reading of the virgin birth, seeing it as a supernatural act where the Holy Spirit caused Mary to conceive Jesus without a human father. Matthew recounts, "She was found to be with child from the Holy Spirit" (Matthew 1:18), while Luke describes Mary's own bewilderment:

"How can this be, since I am a virgin?" (Luke 1:34). The angel Gabriel answers, "The Holy Spirit will come upon you, and the power of the Most High will overshadow you" (Luke 1:35). This view emphasizes that the event was not just unusual, but outside normal human experience—a <u>direct intervention by God</u>.

For believers who hold to this interpretation, the virgin birth matters for central doctrines. It signals Jesus' dual identity: <u>from divine source and fully human</u>. By bypassing ordinary conception, Jesus' birth is seen as free from inherited sin, supporting the foundation of Christ's sinless life and unique role as Savior. The virgin birth, then, serves as a marker of Jesus' singular mission and as evidence of God acting in unprecedented ways within human history. – (*J. Gresham Machen, Readings and Analysis*). This understanding finds continuity in Old Testament promises, where Isaiah writes, *"The virgin will conceive and give birth to a son, and will call him Immanuel"* – (**Isaiah 7:14**), linking prophetic hope with the events in Nazareth.

POSSIBILITY OF INTERPRETATION 2:

Symbolic or Theological Interpretations

Some modern Christians and biblical scholars approach the virgin birth as a rich theological narrative rather than a literal biological account. This view focuses on what the story means about God, Jesus, and faith, rather than insisting every detail reflects physical reality. In this interpretive model, the story conveys spiritual truths: Jesus' unique calling, the nearness of God to ordinary people, and the mystery of divine action in the world.

Supporters of a symbolic understanding note that ancient writers often used birth narratives to highlight someone's importance or special mission. They argue that, for the earliest Christians, describing Jesus' birth in miraculous terms expressed convictions about his divine origin and God's commitment to Israel and the world. The story's value, in this view, lies more in what it communicates about God's initiative and Jesus' divine purpose than in its explanation of physical processes. - (Wahlberg, 2020). This approach allows faith to engage with scientific knowledge about human reproduction, seeing the biblical account as a way of expressing profound truths about Jesus' significance using the language and symbols of the time.

POSSIBILITY OF INTERPRETATION 3:

Naturalistic or Scientific Perspectives

Other interpreters start with skepticism about supernatural events and read the virgin birth story through the lens of history, culture, and science. Some suggest Mary's pregnancy may have had natural causes, unknown to ancient people, or that the story arose to resolve social difficulties or strengthen Jesus' credentials among his followers. The idea that Mary conceived by the Spirit may have helped early Christians respond to questions or rumors, especially as the new movement moved beyond its original Jewish setting.

Historical critics sometimes argue that birth narratives developed over time to make sense of Jesus' authority and spiritual power, echoing how ancient biographies of other important figures sometimes featured unusual or miraculous births. - (Wahlberg, 2020). While these explanations are not accepted by those holding traditional Christian beliefs, they raise questions about how stories function in shaping faith identity, and what it means to say a text is inspired, true, or trustworthy.

Combined Implications for Faith and Doctrine

These three approaches—literal, symbolic, and naturalistic—open different paths for understanding one of Christianity's most distinctive claims. Treating the virgin birth as a supernatural fact supports traditional views about Jesus' divinity, his fulfillment of prophecy, and the uniqueness of God's saving work in history. Viewing it as theological symbolism creates room for conversation between faith and contemporary science, highlighting spiritual meaning over physical mechanism while still honoring the text's message. Taking a naturalistic approach often challenges established doctrine, prompting deeper reflection on why such stories matter and what makes them powerful for generations of believers.

The virgin conception story, **rare** and <u>debated</u> as it is, invites everyone—whether convinced, questioning, or simply curious—to consider what it means for God to act, what it means for Jesus to be unique, and how ancient texts continue to shape both belief and life's most important questions. – (*J. Gresham Machen, Readings and Analysis*, 2025; Wahlberg, 2020). Tension among these views keeps the discussion alive for modern readers.

José E. Espinoza

Summary and Reflection of Chapter 2

Having explored the historical setting, cultural challenges, and various interpretations of **Mary's virgin conception**, we now stand at a crossroads of faith and understanding. This remarkable event continues to invite us into deeper reflection on how God's power can move beyond human expectations and natural laws, shaping both the story of Jesus and the foundation of Christian belief. Whether viewed as a <u>literal miracle</u>, a <u>powerful symbol</u>, or <u>a subject of critical inquiry</u>, the virgin birth challenges us to consider what it means for God to enter the world in surprising ways. With this knowledge, we can approach the Gospels with fresh eyes, ready to engage thoughtfully with the mysteries they hold and to guide others in exploring their significance for faith today.

Reference List of Chapter 2

Primary Biblical Reference:

Matthew 1:18 The <u>Rare Pregnancy of Mary</u>; (Not Man Sperm involved) **Conceiving Jesus** <u>by the power of the Holy Spirit</u> **while she was still a virgin**. … *"while she was still a virgin, she became pregnant through the power of the Holy Spirit."* **According to (the Bible) – New Living Translation. – And other Versions such as NKJ & NIV…etc.**

Other References:

Matthew 1 - Dr. Constable's Expository Notes - Bible Commentaries - StudyLight.org. (2025). - StudyLight.org.

J. Gresham Machen, Readings and Analysis. (2025, May 24). - thereligionthatstartedinahat.org

MATTHEW 01:18-25: GOD'S INTERVENTION IN THE BIRTH OF JESUS | Bible interpretation by Fr. Abraham Mutholath. (2024). - bibleinterpretation.org.

Wahlberg, M. (2020, July 17). *Divine Revelation* (E. N. Zalta, Ed.). Stanford Encyclopedia of Philosophy; - Metaphysics Research Lab, Stanford University. – stanford.edu

Chapter 3:

Rare Case of...

An ANGEL in DREAMS

**'Divine Messenger' Instructing a Man
What to Do While This Man Sleeps**

<u>Matthew 1:20 - 25</u> ... "An <u>Angel</u> of the Lord <u>Appears to Joseph</u> in a Dream"; ('not name of the Angel') Telling him what to do. – (Bible) – New Living Translation.

The Angel with Joseph and Divine Guidance at Night

Have you ever wondered how a quiet moment in the night could change the course of history? What might it mean when an angel appears not in broad daylight but **in a dream**, delivering <u>a message that calls for trust and obedience amid confusion</u>? Why would God choose to speak through such a private, still encounter rather than a public sign or bold declaration? These questions invite us to explore a unique story tucked within the **Gospel of Matthew 1:20** where divine guidance comes gently yet powerfully <u>to a man wrestling with uncertainty</u>. As we reflect on this **rare nighttime visitation**, we'll discover how a single dream carries weight far beyond its moment, offering insight into faith, courage, and God's timing that resonates across generations.

The Phenomenon of Dreams and Angels in relation to Joseph's Narrative

Dreams hold a special place in the biblical story. Throughout Scripture, God uses dreams as a way to send critical instructions, comfort, warnings, and new directions. Sometimes, these dreams come when daytime distractions vanish and when the sleeper needs reassurance or clarity. One striking example is the **dream Joseph experiences** in **Matthew 1:20**, when <u>an angel brings a life-altering message</u> that alters the direction of the Holy Family and, with it, the <u>course of redemption history</u> for humanity.

Joseph <u>faces a moment of intense tension</u>. **He knows Mary is pregnant**, <u>but not by him</u>, and under the Mosaic Law, his options are both public and private, with great cost attached either way. Out of compassion, Joseph plans a private separation out of respect for Mary's reputation. This decision already reflects a heart open to mercy and humility. - (*The Gospel of Matthew - Wesley Scott Amos Ministries*, 2025). Then, in the stillness of sleep, the course changes. God intervenes with **a message** not shouted from a public stage, but given <u>quietly through a dream</u>, **using an angel** as <u>the messenger</u>.

Dreams represent a trusted channel for divine communication, particularly when the message involves personal situations brimming with vulnerability or possible shame. This pattern appears elsewhere in Scripture. **For example**, God gives <u>Jacob dreams</u> at turning points in Genesis, such as the ladder at Bethel. <u>Pharaoh in Egypt</u> receives warning dreams that <u>Joseph interprets</u>, saving nations from famine. **<u>Daniel receives dreams</u>** full of complex images and visions, <u>revealing the rise and fall of empires</u>. Yet, 'these often involve symbolism or demand an interpreter'. When God chooses to speak directly through a dream without an interpreter, as in the case of Joseph, the effect is heightened—it shows both the urgency of the moment and God's respect for the individual receiving the message.

<u>The angelic visitation to Joseph</u> stands apart as **a rare and striking event**. Many biblical dreams communicate truth using symbols, but few feature an angel appearing **with such direct instructions**. <u>The angel is, interestingly, left unnamed</u>, unlike Gabriel who appears to Mary and Zechariah elsewhere. This detail directs attention away from the identity or stature of the messenger and toward the substance of the message itself. Unlike visions granted to the prophets in the daylight, which often come with a crowd or a scribe to record and share, this meeting is private, shrouded in the mystery of night. **God honors Joseph with** both <u>a dramatic revelation and an invitation into a quiet partnership</u>.

God's trust in Joseph shows up through the deeply personal approach. **The message is** not a broad announcement but **a mission**. <u>The angel guides Joseph to take Mary as his wife</u>, explains the miraculous conception by the Holy Spirit, and <u>provides Joseph with the authority</u>

to name the child Jesus. The timing matters: Joseph receives his instruction before he can act out of pain, frustration, or perceived betrayal. The angel's words push back on Joseph's fear, inviting him to lay aside suspicion and step forward in obedience. - (*The Gospel of Matthew - Wesley Scott Amos Ministries*, 2025). This act roots Joseph within God's redemptive plan while providing assurance at a moment when confusion and heartbreak loom.

This message accomplishes more than announcing a birth—it prevents Joseph from quietly ending the relationship, secures Mary and Jesus' reputation, and upholds the fulfillment of Scripture. **Joseph's response models** what Evangelical Christian scholarship often highlights: the call to trust, obey, and receive God's direction, even in confusing and uncharted times. **The angel's visit is a safeguard** for the holy family, but also for the integrity of God's larger promise stretching from the prophets to Messiah.

Joseph's experience stands within a broader biblical pattern. God's guidance often comes in moments of uncertainty. In the Old Testament, God spoke in the night to Samuel with guidance for Israel. In Daniel, dreams interpret destinies. In this lineage, Joseph's dream brings protection when his own plans would have missed the mark. For Evangelical Christan readers, this signals that **God's communication is active and personal**— it arrives in unexpected ways and often meets us in vulnerable places. Divine guidance sometimes requires a quiet heart, an open mind, and willingness to suspend judgment.

Interpretive Analysis: Readings of the Angel's Message with Scriptural Reinforcement

Experiences of divine encounter often arrive in quiet moments, dreamlike and unannounced, as with Joseph's night visitation. **These rare stories** of angelic guidance in the Gospels invite personal engagement for everyone wrestling with questions of faith, doubt, and direction. Moving from the historical and narrative details, the story now calls for deeper reflection on **what Joseph's dream encounter with the angel means** <u>for those walking the Christian path today</u>.

POSSIBILITY OF INTERPRETATION 1:

Divine Assurance of God's Plan

Joseph finds himself in the grip of fear and confusion as he discovers that Mary, his betrothed or engaged wife to be, is expecting a child. Under ordinary circumstances, he would have been justified in stepping away, but God speaks directly into his anxiety: *"Do not be afraid to take Mary as your wife"* - (**Matthew 1:20**, NLT). In this moment, God reassures Joseph that what seems a crisis—an unexplainable and **rare event** outside normal expectations—is actually part of divine orchestration. Joseph is given a front-row seat to a supernatural work far <u>beyond his understanding</u>. This same dynamic plays out in the lives of many who feel trapped between what they know of faith and what their situation seems to demand. **God's message—do not be afraid—carries across centuries**, reassuring all who battle unease or the threat of social scrutiny. Situations at work, family decisions, or moves to new towns can unsettle the heart, but this account from Matthew affirms God's sovereignty, reminding believers that his purposes continue even when the path is shadowed by doubt or public misunderstanding.

POSSIBILITY OF INTERPRETATION 2:

Model of Discernment and Obedience

Joseph models a posture of quiet discernment, showing that following God's leading sometimes means taking action without external confirmation or applause. The text gives a simple but powerful account: *"...And Joseph did as the angel of the Lord commanded him..."* - (**Matthew 1:24**, NLT). Joseph chooses trust over hesitation, acting in faith rather than seeking validation from others. He does not wait for further dreams, signs, or explanations—**he obeys**. This approach offers guidance today for discerning God's voice amid the noise of competing opinions. In vocational matters, a believer may sense God nudging them toward a new area of service or workplace role, even if it contradicts personal plans or lacks public support. A young adult wrestling with relationship choices might feel called to wait, move forward, or hold steady—never with a billboard announcement, but with peace in prayer. Ministry callings often arrive as quiet conviction to care for the overlooked, serve in less-visible ways, or step into responsibility that others may not understand. Joseph's response shows humility and a heart tuned to God, inviting readers to value internal conviction formed through prayer and scripture above popular sentiment.

POSSIBILITY OF INTERPRETATION 3:

Validation of Jesus' Divine Origin

Beyond personal encouragement and practical modeling, the angel's message to Joseph affirms one of Christianity's core beliefs—the divine conception and mission of Jesus. **The angel's words** frame <u>Mary's child as unique, set apart by God's special purpose:</u> ***"She will*** *have a son, and you are to name him <u>Jesus</u>, for <u>he will save his people from their sins.</u>"* - (**Matthew 1:21**, NLT). Joseph becomes both legal father and guardian, safeguarding the miraculous child whose arrival fulfills ancient prophecy. **The dream**, then, <u>isn't simply about Joseph's reputation or family honor</u>; **it is a cornerstone in God's entrance into human story**, demonstrating that Jesus is not the product of human planning or error, but the **fulfillment of salvation's promise**. This interpretation matters for Christian readers wrestling with questions of identity and assurance: **Jesus** is not only a historical figure or moral teacher, but <u>the Son of God entering the world to deliver salvation</u>. Trust in the angel's message means embracing the miraculous heart of the Christian story and realizing that faith centers on Jesus' identity and purpose.

ADITIONAL POSSIBILITY OF INTERPRETATION

Invitation to Trust God's Timing and Purpose

Joseph's response is not just about believing the message, but embracing a new path, <u>even when understanding remains incomplete</u>. *"When Joseph woke up, he did as the angel of the Lord commanded."* - (Matthew 1:24, NLT). The narrative doesn't report lengthy deliberations or public speeches. **Joseph simply steps into the story**

God is writing. Faith here is not passive; it is a <u>willingness to act promptly</u> even when divine timing disrupts personal plans and schedules. Many Christians know this struggle: waiting for God's answer, feeling discomfort as life veers away from expectations, or stepping forward despite unanswered questions. Whether facing decisions about education, career, marriage, or serving in new contexts, this encounter calls readers to rest in God's wisdom and move forward in trust, even when it means adjusting to timing and circumstances beyond personal preference.

Each <u>interpretation</u>—divine assurance, <u>discernment and obedience</u>, <u>affirmation of Jesus' identity</u>, <u>invitation to patient faith</u>—offers a window into the spiritual richness of Joseph's dream. This episode isn't just a story from the past, but a lived **invitation for today's readers to discern**, <u>trust, and obey</u> the quiet voice of God through every uncertainty and change.

Summary and Reflection of Chapter 3

Now that we have explored the rare and powerful angelic visitation to Joseph, we can see how this quiet moment in the night holds deep meaning for our own journeys of faith. Joseph's experience shows us that God often speaks in unexpected ways—through dreams, silence, or personal conviction—and calls us to trust and obey even when the path is unclear. His story encourages us to listen carefully for God's voice, to move forward with courage despite uncertainty, and to embrace the unfolding of God's plan with patience and hope. As we reflect on Joseph's obedience and the angel's message, we are invited to deepen our faith, remain open to divine guidance, and share these lessons with others who seek encouragement in their own walk with God.

Reference List of Chapter 3:

Primary Biblical Reference:

Matthew 1:20 "An Angel of the Lord Appears to Joseph in a Dream"; 'not name of the Angel' Mentioned – (Bible) – New Living Translation.

Other References:

Matthew 1. (2024). - netbible.org

The Gospel of Matthew - Wesley Scott Amos Ministries. (2025). - wesleyscottamos.com

Part 2:

RARITY Of...

A NEW KINGDOM

Chapter 4:

Rare Case of…

A "Born KING"

Royalty In A Person; Declared King at Birth, Unlike Any Other

<u>Matthew 2: 2</u> – NKJV, – NIV.
"Where Is <u>He Who Has Been Born King</u>?"

José E. Espinoza

The <u>RARE</u> and Unusual <u>BORN KING</u>;

Mentioned in <u>Matthew 2: 2</u>

"Where is he who has been born king of the Jews?" This simple question, spoken by strangers from distant lands, carries a weight far greater than just curiosity. It touches on hopes, fears, and deep expectations rooted **in a complex world of politics, religion, and power**. In a time when kings meant conquest or control, the idea of a new king was anything but ordinary—it sparked anxiety for rulers and stirred the longing of oppressed people. Yet, beneath this tension lies a mystery: <u>**what kind of king** could be born into such uncertainty</u>? The question invites us to explore not only the political and historical backdrop but also the surprising ways **this king's reign challenges common ideas about power and authority**. As we reflect on this moment, we begin to see a story that crosses boundaries—of nations, traditions, and even our own understanding of leadership and hope.

Context and Historical Setting: The Messianic and Political Expectations of <u>Matthew 2:2</u>

In the first century, <u>Jewish society lived under a restless expectation for a Messiah</u> who would free them from Roman oppression. Centuries of foreign empires had ruled over Judea, leaving a longing for national independence. Prophets from the Hebrew Scriptures had painted hopeful visions of a deliverer, **someone from David's royal line** who would restore Israel's fortune. When the Magi arrived from the East, asking, *"**Where is he who <u>has been born king</u>** of the Jews?"* they did more than note a royal birth; <u>their question echoed a dream carried for generations</u>: the hope for a king who would restore sovereignty to Israel. Words like *"king of the Jews"* were filled with possibility and risk. Even those outside the Jewish faith recognized that such an announcement could spark tremendous change. The question the Magi posed, then, carried a weight that was religious, cultural, and political all at once. - (*The Visit by the Magi in **<u>Matthew 2:1-12</u>***). History had shown that rumors of a Messiah could ignite revolts and were feared by both Rome and those who ruled under its watch.

King Herod the Great sat uneasily on the Judean throne. An Edomite by birth, propped up by Roman power, Herod's authority was a fragile arrangement resented by many of his subjects. He viewed himself as the legitimate ruler, yet every movement—every murmur among the people—threatened his claim. Herod was known for his paranoia and cruelty, even to his own family. - (Guzik, 2015). For him, the notion of a child *"born King of the Jews"* implied a **legitimate royal** rival, not a king in **title** only, but one whose blood and birth claimed **authority** Herod could never possess. This wasn't just a theological issue. Any suggestion that an heir to David's throne had arrived was an act of sedition. In the delicate system of Roman governorship, a rumor about a new king could unsettle the status quo and invite Roman intervention. Herod's later violence revealed how such a claim touched the heart of insecurity for a regime built on compromise and external approval. The Magi's question, therefore, threatened the delicate balance of local politics and imperial rule, sending ripples of unease through Jerusalem. It wasn't just Herod who was troubled—the whole city sensed the danger of another messianic claim.

The idea of a *"born king"* drew deep from Old Testament promises. Scriptures like **Psalm 2** spoke of God's Anointed ruling with power, subduing the nations, and establishing a **reign that brought justice** and blessings. **Isaiah described a child born whose government and peace would have no end**, seated on David's throne. These pictures shaped the hope of the people, nurturing a conviction that **a true king** would arise who embodied both mercy and might. Matthew's Gospel draws on these prophecies to show that Jesus did not merely take the title of king—he embodied the promises and expectations of Israel. - (Guzik, 2015; *The Visit by the Magi in Matthew 2:1-12*, 2015). Yet, the story resists the straightforward fulfillment that many imagined.

Instead of leading a rebellion or waging battle, **Jesus' kingship began in humility and vulnerability**. In Matthew, the child is found not in a palace but in an ordinary home, surrounded by worship and curiosity, not conquest and acclaim. This contrast—between popular expectation and actual manifestation—raises questions about authority, power, and the kind of kingdom that was truly coming into the world.

It stands out that <u>the first to recognize</u> the birth of this king were not Jewish leaders or priests, but <u>Magi from distant lands</u>. Their journey bridges worlds—travelers from the East, students of stars, drawn by a sign that pointed to something beyond their own traditions. They arrive in Jerusalem asking for a king, not just of the Jews, but a figure whose arrival matters far beyond one ethnic group or territory. Their actions suggest that <u>this new king's significance would reach into unexpected places</u>. Their willingness to respond and worship demonstrates a hope that surpasses boundaries of nation and background. - (*Matthew 2:1-12*). At a time when power and privilege were usually kept within narrow circles, the Magi's appearance startled the city. Their question combined wonder and reverence, but it also carried uncertainty—**what sort of king** was being announced here, and <u>what would it mean for the world</u> around them?

All these tensions—the longing for deliverance, the fear of rivals, the anticipation of prophecy, and the surprise of foreign recognition—come together in a single, searching question. Readers can sense how loaded these words were in their original time: ***"Where is he who has***

José E. Espinoza

been born king of the Jews?" The mention of a **"born king"** was neither ordinary nor safe. Every listener and reader was left to ponder <u>what sort of king was truly being spoken about</u>, and what shape his kingship might ultimately take. These questions linger, inviting reflection on what it meant—and still means—to call **Jesus** a **king**.

Interpretive Possibilities and Theological Angles: Three Readings of the 'Born King'

POSSIBILITY OF INTERPRETATION 1:

The Humble King: <u>Royalty</u> in <u>Unexpected</u> Form

Jesus' coming as king stands out because he appears not in the splendor of a palace, but in the ordinariness of a manger. - **(Luke 2:7)**. Matthew's Gospel presents Jesus' kingship as rooted in humility, a pattern that runs against the grain of the ancient world, where royal figures seized power with armies or inherited thrones through bloodlines and political intrigue. **In contrast**, Jesus' birth takes place in Bethlehem, far from royal courts, attended by shepherds, not nobility. His authority arises not from force or privilege, but from self-giving love. Even as the magi recognize his kingship in Matthew 2:2, Jesus remains a child, vulnerable and defenseless, whose life and reign are marked by serving others - (Matthew 20:28) and associating with outcasts and the marginalized.

This humble kingship continues through Jesus' actions—washing his disciples' feet, touching lepers, and welcoming children. He often instructs his followers that greatness in his kingdom means becoming "least". - (Matthew 18:4). **The king's crown** is eventually <u>one of thorns</u>, and his throne (of power and triumph) is an instrument of execution (the cross) - (Matthew 27:29, Matthew 27:37). For many evangelical readers, this radical image redefines authority and leadership. Jesus models a rule where power serves, not dominates, and calls disciples to imitate a way of self-sacrifice instead of self-aggrandizement. Instead of launching a kingdom by military campaign or political decree, Jesus changes the world through humility and redemptive suffering, opening space for reflection about how real strength often looks like weakness according to the values of the world. - (*Matthew 2 Commentary | Precept Austin*, n.d.). This understanding leads to a vision of the kingdom shaped by inner transformation and spiritual renewal, rather than conquest or borders.

POSSIBILITY OF INTERPRETATION 2:

Prophetic <u>Fulfillment</u>: <u>Jesus</u> as the <u>Promised Davidic King</u>

Matthew's story links Jesus to **promises made to David** centuries earlier. The phrase "king of the Jews" resonates with texts like **<u>Jeremiah 23:5</u>**, which speaks of a righteous <u>descendant from David's line who will reign as king and bring justice</u>. In **2 Samuel 7:12-16**, God commits to establish <u>David's throne forever through his offspring</u>. For the gospel's first readers, this connection meant Jesus was not a mere spiritual visionary, but **the actual, promised king** sent <u>to inaugurate God's reign on earth</u> and restore Israel's hopes. - (*Myth and History in the Epiphany of Matthew 2 | Psephizo*, 2021). By tracing Jesus' genealogy back to David - (Matthew 1:1-17) and placing his birth in Bethlchem - (<u>Micah 5:2</u> adapted in <u>Matthew 2:5-6</u>), <u>Matthew crafts a portrait</u> of **Jesus** as the **long-awaited fulfillment of messianic prophecy**.

This interpretive lens sees Jesus as the true, divinely-appointed successor to David—one who establishes a kingdom marked by God's justice, peace, and faithfulness. His authority is not invented by Matthew or shaped by wishful thinking, but anchored in ancient covenants. His kingship is trustworthy because **it emerges from a**

consistent divine plan, and for evangelical faith, seeing **Jesus** as the Davidic **King** reveals God's faithfulness to fulfill every promise. - (*Matthew 2 Commentary | Precept Austin*, n.d.). **This recognition shapes Christian understanding of the Bible**, presenting **Jesus Christ** as the thread weaving Old and New Testaments together.

POSSIBILITYOF INTERPRETATION 3:

A Controversial Claim: Political Threat and Divine Mystery

Calling **Jesus "king"** stirred fear and anxiety in the world he entered. Matthew describes Herod's alarm when magi announce a rival king, igniting fierce opposition and violence - (**Matthew 2:3-16**). Herod's massacre of children in Bethlehem shows how claims about Jesus threaten political power and expose the tensions between human rulers and God's sovereignty. Some interpreters see in this story a **collision of two kingdoms**: one built on violence and manipulation, the other on divine mystery and grace.

This framework highlights the lived reality of discipleship under contested authority. **Jesus' kingship continually provokes unrest**, not only in Herod's household, but throughout his life, as seen in conflicts with religious leaders and, later, Rome's soldiers at the cross.

He does not raise an army, yet his life and message undermine false allegiances and expose the limits of earthly power. When believers claim allegiance to **Jesus as king**, they participate in a story that resists compromise with powers that oppose God's purposes, calling for courage, discernment, and sacrifice. - (*Myth and History in the Epiphany of Matthew 2 | Psephizo*, 2021; *Matthew 2 Commentary | Precept Austin*, n.d.). Christian reflection from this angle focuses on how following Christ often means challenging oppressive structures, risking misunderstanding, and witnessing to a kingdom "not of this world," (but it is in this world) and it is determined to influence and take charge.

ADITIONAL POSSIBILITY OF INTERPRETATION

The Universal King: Crossing Boundaries and Nations

The arrival of the magi from "the East" signals that this king's reign is not confined to Israel. **Foreigners recognizing Jesus as king hints at a much broader story—one where God's purposes embrace every nation.** Matthew's Gospel ends with <u>**Jesus declaring**</u>, *"**All authority** <u>in heaven and on earth</u> **has been given to me**"*. - (Matthew

28:18), pointing to a vision of **kingship that reaches across cultures, languages, and territories**.

This perspective suggests Jesus' birth carries cosmic implications, making him king for all people, not just for one tribe or tradition. In Christian practice, this universal vision propels mission work, cross-cultural partnership, and the call for the church to welcome those from every background. The magi's gifts and worship become signs of a future where every people and language celebrate Jesus' reign, shaping both theology and practice for a truly global Christian movement, and The Kingdom of God proclaimed and expanded throughout the entire planet earth.

Summary and Reflection of Chapter 4

Having explored the historical, political, and theological layers behind the title **"King"** in Matthew 2:2, we see that Jesus' kingship challenges expectations of <u>power, authority, and identity</u>. The question posed by the Magi invites us to consider a king who is at once humble and prophetic, **controversial** and universal—one whose reign reshapes what it means to lead and rule. Now that we understand these rich dimensions, we can approach this passage with fresh curiosity and deeper insight, ready to engage others in conversations about **Jesus' unique role as King** and what his story **<u>reveals</u>** about **God's Kingdom breaking into our world**.

Reference List of Chapter 4:

Primary Biblical Reference

Matthew 2: 2 *"Where Is He Who Has Been Born King?"* According to; the - Bible New King James Version

Other References

Guzik, D. (2015, December 8). *Matthew Chapter 2*. - EnduringWord.com

Myth and history in the Epiphany of Matthew 2 | Psephizo. (2021, December 29). – Psphizo.com

Matthew 2 Commentary | Precept Austin. (n.d.). - preceptaustin.org

The Visit by the Magi in Matthew 2:1-12. (2015, December 27). Reflections on Theological Topics of Interest. – Regehrlein.Wordpress.com

Chapter 5:

Rare Case of…

STAR that Move & Stop

Defying Constellations Norm and Stablished Principle

<u>Matthew 2:2</u>, and <u>Matthew 2:9</u> According to; the Bible – New Living Translation

José E. Espinoza

Miracle, Symbol, or Astronomical Event?

The **rare story of the moving star** in the New Testament challenges everything we think we know about signs in the sky. Unlike ordinary stars that follow predictable paths, **this star seems to defy natural laws—it guides travelers over a specific route and stops exactly where their journey ends**. For centuries, scholars and believers alike have debated whether this event was a literal miracle, a symbolic message, or simply an unusual astronomical occurrence misunderstood by ancient observers. This chapter invites you to examine the biblical story alongside historical and scientific perspectives, opening the door to fresh ways of understanding one of the Gospel's most puzzling and intriguing details.

Biblical Description, Ancient Context, and Natural Phenomena Candidates

A star rises in the east, shining with an unusual brilliance. **Wise men—** trained in ancient astronomy—notice its ascent. They travel far, speaking of *"his star when it rose"* and searching for a newborn king - (**Matthew 2:2**). Their journey does not follow vague stargazing, but a light that, according to the narrative, *"went before them"* and then stopped above the exact place the child was (**Matthew 2:9**). This detail leaps out: ordinary stars do not travel across the sky guiding specific travelers, then halt precisely over one house. Since ancient times, this story has pulled at minds both curious and learned, raising a puzzle that spans the disciplines of theology, astronomy, and history.

For the people of Matthew's era, wonders in the night sky were nothing new. Civilizations like Babylon and Persia developed sophisticated ways of tracking planets, stars, and the occasional comet. The Magi who appear in the Gospel narrative most likely belonged to this world—**priests or wise** men steeped in their culture's astrological traditions. Using careful records on clay tablets, skilled astronomers charted planetary paths, predicted eclipses, and read omens in the heavens. **They recognized rare events**: a bright alignment of planets, the sweep of a comet, the sudden appearance of a nova. Each of these natural phenomena inspired awe, often treated as signs that powerful events were unfolding on earth.

The Gospel account adds a twist. **The "star"** in Matthew's text performs unheard-of feats. It moves not simply with the sky's normal arc, but guides from Jerusalem south to Bethlehem—about six miles—**leading wise men to a house and then stopping over it**. No celestial object observed in antiquity had ever behaved like this. Planets move along set paths, stars rise in the east and set in the west, and even the grandest comet cannot pinpoint a location for travelers to visit. Matthew's phrasing highlights the wonder: **the light goes**

"before them," acting more like a personal guide than a distant astronomical body.

Scholars have explored natural explanations closely, proposing several candidates for the star. Some point to planetary conjunctions, especially the triple meeting of Jupiter and Saturn in 7 BC. To the trained eyes of Babylonian or Persian astrologers, such an event would have carried weighty meaning. Jupiter—the "star of the universe"—combining forces with Saturn, linked to Palestine, in the constellation of Pisces, a harbinger of last days, might have sent **a clear message of 'an epoch-making' royal birth**. - (admin, 2015). Observing the night sky, ancient priests would have seen the planets' glow merge, forming a striking "star" visible over months. Yet even devoted observers knew these were movements governed by natural law. Such conjunctions, while rare, occurred at intervals and couldn't stop over a house or travel short distances from town to town.

Other proposals focus on comets or novae. Sometimes a comet blazes for weeks, its tail arcing across familiar skies. A nova, an explosion of a distant star, can also create a dazzling point of sudden light. Ancient records describe these events—Chinese astronomers in particular chronicled "guest stars" unexpected in the night. Both phenomena, however, come with problems. Natural objects move steadily across the sky. They do not pause in place or "lead" people through a landscape. The story in Matthew resists being confined to what ancient naturalists could explain.

Because standard explanations falter, another framework emerges: the star as a supernatural sign. This reading accepts the event as one that defies nature—not a comet, not a rare planetary crossing, but <u>a phenomenon brought about by God's intervention</u>. The star functions as a visible pointer, guiding the Magi on a journey no simple calculation could predict. From 'the pillar of fire' during the Exodus to the 'blaze of light' on the road to Damascus, <u>the biblical record often connects God's activity with wondrous or miraculous radiance</u>. **The "star"** in Matthew <u>acts as a personal escort</u>, leading the Magi step by step, then stopping above the child, **signaling** that <u>divine power was at work in this moment of history</u>.

Ancient readers, and their modern counterparts, have struggled with this tension: are we witnessing a rare masterpiece of timing in the heavens, a carefully arranged series of astronomical wonders, or a miracle that transcends the motions of sun, planets, and stars? The biblical text invites curiosity by describing a light that refuses to fit neatly into the patterns of ordinary observation. Those who look closely are left with a question—the same question that urged the Magi onward: What kind of sign could draw wise men from afar and point so clearly to a newborn king?

Interpretive Frameworks and Theological Relevance

Questions about the star that led the Magi never quite fit into one box. The event lives at the crossroads of miracle, message, nature, and culture. Approaching it through the frameworks people have used to explain the story opens up layers of meaning that continue to shape Christian belief and imagination.

POSSIBILITY OF INTERPRETATION 1:

Literal Miracle Interpretation

For many, the Gospel expects the reader to see the star as a **supernatural** intervention—God bending the physical world to lead gentle seekers to Jesus. This reading takes the narrative at face value: the star does something no known astronomical object does, traveling ahead of the Magi, stopping over a house, displaying willful movement. People holding this view, point to the precedent of signs and wonders throughout Scripture, seeing the star as part of God's direct action in salvation history. - (Armstrong, 2021). Theologically, this interpretation makes a clear declaration: **God is not limited by natural law** but reigns as both **Creator** and **Sustainer**, able at any moment to act in ways that leave science speechless. The Magi become witnesses to a truth the Old Testament proclaims often—**God reveals himself, not just in Israel**, but to distant nations. Their arrival, guided by the miraculous star, stands for the gentile world's welcome into the messianic promise. Adherents to this view hold that divine revelation does not need rational validation, and the miraculous **sign of the star demands faith** in God's power and wisdom. Their approach relies on trusting in the biblical account as a unique moment where natural explanation, however attractive, is neither required nor sufficient.

POSIBILITY OF INTERPRETATION 2:

Symbolic Interpretation

Another stream of interpretation considers the star less as a physical object and more as a loaded symbol. Here, the detail about the "moving" star highlights God's purposeful activity but does not necessarily describe a historic astronomical occurrence. The focus switches to what the story proclaims about Jesus—God's true promised king, light sent into a dark world, hope rising over all people. For these interpreters, the journey and adoration of the Magi fulfill Old Testament hopes of nations coming to worship the Lord. - (Adair, 2016). They read the star as another signpost in the Gospel's tapestry of fulfillment, emphasizing meaning over mechanism. The star "stops" because **God's purpose finds its mark**; <u>the Magi's quest ends at the place of God's choosing</u>. This school aligns itself with much of ancient literature, where signs in the sky serve not only to narrate events, but to communicate theological truths about kingship and destiny. Savoring the richness of biblical symbolism, these interpreters encourage a reading that looks past physical details and seeks the spiritual voice of the story. In this way, the star becomes part of the tradition that sees Jesus as the "light to the nations," illuminating the path for all who seek.

POSSIBILITY IF INTERPRETATION 3:

Natural Astronomical Event Interpretation

Many propose the event described in Matthew reflects real phenomena that Mesopotamian sages would have found impressive. Theories range from planetary conjunctions—Jupiter and Saturn, or a series of bright appearances of Jupiter itself—to comets or a possible nova. Ancient records show astrologers assigning meaning to dazzling objects in the night sky. To Magi trained in scanning for meaning among the planets and stars, an unusual appearance could easily spell the birth of a great king. - (Hoffmann, 2021; Armstrong, 2021). Popular versions suggest the "star" was a recognizable event interpreted through the lens of ancient prophecy and astrology. This makes the Magi's journey plausible within their culture: the sky brought messages to those who knew how to read them. Yet, this view faces a sharp question: **how do you explain the star "stopping"** <u>over a specific house</u>? No known buildup or conjunction or comet has the capacity to isolate a single building in a small village. Scholars following this trail often see the biblical language as cultural—phenomenological description and interpretive storytelling rather than precise scientific reporting.

Possibility of Interpretation in Combination

A fourth path tries to hold together the threads of **nature and miracle**. Here, <u>the star was a genuine astronomical event</u>—a planetary alignment or a striking appearance of Jupiter, perhaps—**used by God as a sign**, but with a supernatural "layer" <u>that guided the Magi with precision</u> no natural body could achieve. God sets the ordinary world in motion and, when needed, guides it with extraordinary providence.

The miracle lies not in bending natural law to breaking, but in orchestrating events for a particular purpose that would speak to people attuned to the skies. - (Armstrong, 2021; Adair, 2016). This position honors both an observable phenomenon and God's active direction, showing that faith and empirical inquiry need not stand as rivals. The story then sits comfortably within ancient **Jewish and Christian convictions** that <u>God communicates through both creation and direct intervention</u>.

Evangelical thought often echoes all four views, depending on emphasis. Some champion direct miracle, others symbolism, others the harmony of astronomy and divine purpose, drawing from a long tradition of Christian thinkers who have asked where faith meets fact. - (Armstrong, 2021). Each interpretation brings questions about God's nature, the authority of Scripture, and the relationship between scientific curiosity and spiritual trust. The star's mystery shines on, inviting fresh wonder at an ancient story.

Summary and Reflection of Chapter 5

Having explored the biblical description, historical background, and various interpretations of **the New Testament's moving star**, we see how this remarkable story challenges us to think deeply about the relationship between <u>faith, history, and the natural world</u>. Whether understood as a literal miracle, a rich symbol, a natural event, or a combination of these, the star invites ongoing reflection on **how God reveals** truth through both the seen and unseen. Now that we have examined these perspectives, we can engage confidently in conversations about this ancient sign—encouraging curiosity, honoring mystery, and appreciating the many ways the Gospel speaks to seekers across time and culture. <u>This understanding equips us to lead others</u> thoughtfully through one of the Bible's most rare, fascinating and inspiring passages.

Reference List of Chapter 5:

Primary Biblical Reference:

Matthew 2:2, and **Matthew 2:9** The Rare case of *"the Star moving & stopping"* Mentioned in According to; the Bible – New Living Translation

Other References:

Adair, A. (2016, December 23). *A Critical Look at the History of Interpreting the Star of Bethlehem in Scientific Literature and Biblical Studies.* - Academia.edu

Armstrong, D. (2021, January 13). *Star of Bethlehem: Natural or Supernatural?* Biblical Evidence for Catholicism. – patheos.com

Geating, W. (2016). *The Star of Bethlehem.* - Biblearchaeology.org

admin. (2015, November 25). *Matthew 2:2 – The star of Bethlehem – Walking With Giants.* Walkingwithgiants.net.

Chapter 6:

Rare Case of…

A LIFE FINALE &

Revelation

Seeing The Greatest Prophecy Fulfilled Before Dying

Luke 2:25-26 – NIV

José E. Espinoza

Simeon's Revelation of seeing the Messiah Before Death

Few people ever receive a clear, direct promise from God about something so personal and profound. Yet Simeon was told he would see the Messiah before he died—a promise fulfilled in a moment that changed everything for him. This kind of divine assurance challenges how we understand faith, timing, and hope. It raises questions about how God chooses to reveal Himself and how those revelations shape not only individual lives but also the expectations of entire communities. The story invites us to reflect deeply on what it means to wait faithfully, to recognize God's work when it comes unexpectedly, and to find encouragement in promises kept beyond our own understanding.

Simeon's Prophetic Promise (Luke 2:25–26): Divine Assurance, Unique Timing, Theological Significance, and Pastoral Encouragement

Biblical passages like Simeon's encounter in Luke 2 prompt careful readers to consider what these moments truly mean. Prophetic narratives invite reflection that goes beyond only what happened.

They open doors to explore how God works, how people respond, and how stories shape faith across centuries. Four faithful approaches arise when engaging with the experience of Simeon in the temple.

Literal Divine Promise

Many Evangelical Christians and scholars take this story as a straightforward record of God's direct intervention. According to this reading, God made Simeon a real promise, and that promise was kept in an actual time and place. Luke's Gospel is often praised for including historical details and eyewitness testimony, signaling the author's intent to present true events. **Simeon**, described as a righteous and devout man, waited faithfully in Jerusalem until he **"saw"** the Lord's Christ. The moment that he physically held the infant Jesus and declared, *"My eyes have seen Your salvation,"* is seen as a powerful example that God fulfills even the most personal of promises in a definite, observable way. - (*Prophetic Praise of Simeon*, 2025). Evangelical commentators argue that stories like this one anchor our trust in the Bible's reliability and fuel hope that God will keep every word He has spoken, not only to prophets and patriarchs, but to ordinary people like Simeon. - (*Charles Simeon-Sermons on Luke | Precept Austin*, 2022). Simeon stands as a reminder that God notices individual faithfulness and responds. For readers who feel weary in waiting, this approach strengthens confidence that hope in God is not misplaced, because He acts in history.

Symbolic Spiritual Insight

Some interpreters suggest there is a deeper layer of meaning within Simeon's sight. While the narrative describes a real event, "seeing" the Messiah also points to spiritual perception. According to this view, the Holy Spirit does not only orchestrate events, but enlightens the hearts and minds of people who are open to God's leading. **Simeon**'s ability <u>to recognize the infant as the Christ</u> was not automatic. There may have been many children in the temple that day, yet it was the Spirit's guidance that allowed Simeon to see beyond appearances. - (*Prophetic Praise of Simeon*, 2025). This interpretation draws attention to the difference between physical observation and spiritual understanding. For believers, it is possible to encounter God's presence in ways that cannot be measured by sight alone. Experiences of prayer, worship, or moments of clarity can be ways the Spirit helps people "see" Christ active in their lives. An example for small groups could be inviting participants to share when they felt the presence or leading of God, even when their circumstances looked ordinary. This perspective reminds readers that faith involves an openness to revelation and a posture of readiness to recognize God's action in unexpected places.

Model of Messianic Expectation

Another approach views **Simeon as** a <u>bridge between the hope of ancient Israel and the fulfillment in Jesus</u>. Evangelical scholars note that, for centuries, faithful Jews longed for the *"consolation of Israel"*—a common prayer for the Messiah's arrival was on their lips. - (*Prophetic Praise of Simeon*, 2025). **Simeon, described** as *"waiting for the consolation of Israel,"* becomes an archetype of this long-held hope. His words and actions show a faith anchored in God's promises stretching back to Abraham and David. - (Genesis 22:16-18; Psalm 89; Psalm 132). By announcing that salvation had come for *"all peoples,"* Simeon's testimony embodies the shift from exclusive national expectations to a worldwide invitation in Christ. This reading highlights Simeon as a communal symbol, not just an individual. Bible study leaders can use this interpretation to encourage discussion about how personal stories of waiting and fulfillment echo within the larger storyline of God's people. - (*Charles Simeon-Sermons on Luke | Precept Austin*, 2022). Early Christians would have read his story and felt assurance that their faith had roots in God's ancient covenant, now fulfilled in Jesus.

Personal and Communal Devotional Application

Simeon's experience continues to speak to believers as a picture of patient and hopeful faith. Evangelical devotional writers often explore how his journey models the posture of waiting on God across a lifetime. His willingness to trust God's promise, stay present in worship, and receive new revelation at the right moment offers guidance for anyone walking through a season of uncertainty. The Nunc Dimittis, Simeon's prayer in Luke 2:29-32, has played a role in Christian liturgy for centuries, reflecting the desire for release and peace after recognizing God's salvation. - (*Prophetic Praise of Simeon*, 2025). Youth ministries may use this narrative as a way to help teens recognize that God's timing is not always predictable but is always wise. In small groups, members might share about promises they are waiting for, finding encouragement in Simeon's persistent hope. This approach sees Simeon as an example and companion for all who long for God's faithfulness, both as individuals and communities.

These four readings, while different, provide windows into the richness of Simeon's encounter. Each approach cultivates a fresh understanding, encouraging a mature engagement with faith that honors the many ways God still works in the world. - (*Prophetic Praise of Simeon*, 2025; *Charles Simeon-Sermons on Luke | Precept Austin*, 2022). Exploring them together helps readers appreciate Scripture's depth and invites them to respond in worship, trust, and expectancy.

Interpretive Possibilities for Simeon's Experience: Four Distinct Readings

The experience of Simeon in Luke 2:25–26 has inspired a range of interpretations that shape how believers approach faith, prophecy, and the presence of the Holy Spirit in everyday life. Each interpretive framework brings out a different facet of the story, inviting young adults, Bible study leaders, and faith explorers to encounter Simeon's story in a way that meets their deepest questions and hopes.

POSSIBILITY OF INTERPRETATION 1:

Literal Divine Promise of Seeing the Messiah Before Death

One popular interpretation holds that Simeon's encounter was <u>a literal, historical promise fulfilled by God</u>. Evangelical scholars who take this view stress the real, physical nature of **Simeon's promise**. He was told directly by the Holy Spirit that he would see the Messiah before death, and he did—meeting the infant Jesus in the temple courts exactly as God had said. This approach is reinforced by Charles Simeon's own expository messages, where he points to Simeon's unwavering expectation and the factual, outward fulfillment of the Spirit's pledge. - (*Charles Simeon-Index to Sermons-2 | Precept Austin*, 2015). Evangelical commentators will often quote the text, "my eyes have seen your salvation," to reinforce that faith in God rests not only on metaphorical meaning but on acts in real time and space. Such an interpretation gives confidence to readers who need tangible anchors for belief in biblical prophecy, showing that God's faithfulness is rooted in verifiable action. For those leading Bible studies or wrestling with doubts, this reading offers a powerful sense of security—God keeps His promises exactly and visibly.

POSSIBILITY OF INTERPRETATION 2:

Symbolic Representation of Spiritual Insight and Readiness

Beyond the historical fulfillment, another interpretive lens sees Simeon's "vision" as a matter of spiritual insight empowered by the Holy Spirit. Here, the act of **"seeing" Jesus goes beyond a merely physical encounter**. Some evangelical sources point out that many in the temple that day witnessed the same event, but only Simeon, guided by the Spirit, truly recognized who Jesus was. George Eliot's reflection on experience and doctrine fits here, stressing how truths must become felt realities before transforming lives. - (The Holy Spirit and Christian Experience 0198827784, 9780198827788 - DOKUMEN.PUB, 2020). In this tradition, the Holy Spirit's role is to open spiritual eyes, allowing believers not just to witness events but to understand their meaning. This reading holds special value for youth and faith explorers seeking a faith that moves beyond surface facts to inward conviction. Bible study leaders can guide groups to ask, "Where is the Spirit inviting us to recognize God's work in new ways?" This frame encourages growth in discernment, not just knowledge.

POSSIBILITY OF INTERPRETATION 3:

A Model of Messianic Expectation and Hope in Early Christianity

Simeon's story can also be read as a model for Messianic expectation—a symbol marking the transition from an era of longing to one of fulfillment. For early Christian communities, Simeon embodied Israel's faithful remnant, waiting through silence and persecution for God's promised deliverance. In this view, **the story stands as <u>a bridge connecting 'Old Testament' longing with 'New Testament' arrival</u>**. Charles Simeon's treatment of Old Testament and New Testament links affirms that Simeon's witness "gives every text its due proportion," highlighting continuity and the reliability of God's revealed plan. - (*Charles Simeon-Index to Sermons-2 | Precept Austin*, 2015). Young adults exploring their place in the ongoing story of faith can find hope in Simeon's perseverance and trust. Bible study leaders may use this interpretation to verify that Christian hope does not break with its roots but rises out of centuries of God's active promise-keeping. This sense of shared story helps communities facing doubt or struggle to see themselves as heirs of ancient expectations now realized in Christ.

ADDITIONAL POSSIBILITY OF INTERPRETATION

Personal and Communal Significance in Devotional Practice

Another way believers have engaged with Simeon's encounter is through its personal and communal devotional significance. Simeon is an icon of patient faith, someone who waits faithfully until God's promise is revealed, a journey that many Christians today know firsthand. Devotional writers encourage believers to respond to waiting with hope and trust, echoing sentiments found in George Eliot's depiction of meaningful pastoral care—where truth becomes transformative only when filtered through lived experience. - (The Holy Spirit and Christian Experience - DOKUMEN.PUB, 2020). For those in seasons of uncertainty, Simeon's story invites prayerful trust and the assurance that God's timing does not disappoint. Small groups and individuals can draw strength from reflecting on past faithfulness to fuel hope in the present.

Each interpretation draws fresh meaning from Luke 2:25–26, fitting the needs of readers at different stages. A literal promise speaks to those needing the concrete reliability of biblical events; the spiritual insight approach deepens prayerful discernment; the Messianic model puts readers in continuity with all of God's people; the devotional frame offers patience and comfort for the present. For every reader, Simeon's story remains a guide—a companion through the journey from longing to fulfillment, from promise to joyful realization. - (*Charles Simeon-Index to Sermons-2 | Precept Austin*, 2015; The Holy Spirit and Christian Experience - DOKUMEN.PUB, 2020). Rather than excluding each other, these frameworks can work together, enriching how communities and individuals encounter God's living word.

Summary and Reflection of Chapter 6

Now that we have explored Simeon's unique encounter with Jesus from multiple angles—seeing it as a clear promise from God, a moment of **deep spiritual insight**, a <u>bridge</u> <u>between</u> **old hopes and new fulfillment**, and a source of patient faith—we can appreciate how rich and meaningful this story truly is. Each way of understanding Simeon's experience offers valuable lessons for our own journeys of faith, encouraging us to trust God's timing, remain open to the Spirit's guidance, connect with the broader story of God's people, and find hope in waiting. For young adults, Bible study leaders, and anyone curious about Scripture, this passage invites ongoing reflection and conversation, helping us grow in faith and recognize how God continues to reveal salvation in our lives today.

RARE CASES Book #1

Reference List of Chapter 6:

Primary Biblical Reference:

Luke 2:25-26 – NIV

Simeon's Revelation of seeing the Messiah Before Death

Other references:

Charles Simeon-Sermons on Luke | Precept Austin. (2022). - Preceptaustin.org.

Charles Simeon-Index to Sermons-2 | Precept Austin. (2015). - Preceptaustin.org.

Prophetic Praise of Simeon. (2025). - Zianet.com.

The Holy Spirit and Christian Experience 0198827784, 9780198827788 - DOKUMEN.PUB. (2020). - dokumen.pub

José E. Espinoza

PART 3:

RARE CASES OF...

A NEW LIFE

In The New Testament with Possibilities of Interpretation;

Chapter 7:

Rare Case of…

A 12-Year-Old BOY Declaration

Concerned About God/The Father's Business

Luke 2:49-50 … "I Must Be About My Father's Business": The Twelve-Year-Old Jesus' Declaration and Identity Formation. - According to The Bible - NKJV

An Extraordinary Boy

At twelve years old, a **boy's** world is often filled with routine—school lessons, family obligations, and the slow unfolding of growing up. Yet, imagine this boy stepping into the grand temple in Jerusalem, surrounded by learned teachers, and speaking words that catch everyone off guard: *"I must be about my Father's business."* In that moment, something stirs beyond ordinary childhood curiosity or **eagerness to learn**. This brief statement opens a window onto a complex journey of identity, faith, and purpose. It invites us to pause and consider what it means for a young person to claim such a close, personal connection with God amid the traditions and expectations of first-century Jewish life. The tensions, questions, and mysteries wrapped up in those few words linger—not just between a child and his parents, but between the human and the divine, the known and the unknown. As we reflect on this encounter, we are drawn into the quiet unfolding of an extraordinary life marked by both growth and deep awareness, challenging us to explore how early moments can reveal far more than they first appear.

Jewish Context and Filial Language in Luke 2:49–50

Jewish society in the first century carried a shared reverence for God framed around the covenant language rooted in Jewish scripture. The term **"Father"** reflected the collective, <u>covenantal bond between God and Israel</u>, distinct from the intimate, individual address that emerges from Jesus at the age of twelve. In synagogue prayers and temple liturgies, Israelites acknowledged the Creator as their Father in a broad sense, locating their identity within the promises to Abraham, Isaac, and Jacob. **When Jesus**, a mere boy, <u>refers to God</u> as *"my Father,"* <u>he distinguishes himself from other Jewish children</u> not just in language but <u>in the depth of relationship implied</u>. His statement goes beyond the customary reverence for God as the nation's Father. Scholars emphasize this shift, explaining that Jesus's words in **Luke 2:49** set a fresh precedent for how early Christian audiences perceived the temple and the presence of God. - (aaron, 2010). It points to a closeness and personal awareness not recognized in childhood prayers or rituals of the time.

A boy's twelfth year in Jewish tradition marked more than the threshold into adolescence. **At this age**, boys entered <u>a period of focused preparation for **Bar Mitzvah**</u>—typically <u>celebrated at thirteen</u>—where they accepted the yoke of the Torah and began to participate fully in communal worship. From morning prayers to attendance at synagogue, twelve-year-olds learned to recite portions of scripture, question teachers, and grasp the legal obligations expected of an adult male within the community. The transition from child to responsible community member was a process unfolding through examples set by family and community elders. A twelve-year-old's religious training often included active participation in feasts, journeys to Jerusalem for major festivals, and practical instruction from scribes or teachers of the Law. In this setting, Jesus's presence in the temple, engaging with Jerusalem's learned teachers and asking questions, fits the pattern of **a boy on the eve of adulthood**. And yet his reply to Mary and Joseph seeps with self-understanding that surpasses ordinary religious enthusiasm. While his peers learned the Law as children of Israel, **Jesus speaks** as one uniquely aware of a direct calling and identity sourced in the heavenly Father.

The temple's significance framed every moment of this encounter. In Jerusalem, the temple stood as the axis mundi—the central location of God's presence, worship, and atonement. Here the people offered sacrifices, marked major festivals, and looked to the priests for guidance. For Jewish families, surrounding the temple with honor was woven into the pattern of yearly rituals such as Passover, which Jesus and his family had just observed. **Observing Jesus in deep discussion with temple teachers** echoes the lived experience of erudite youth soaking up scriptural wisdom, but it also hints at a deeper preoccupation. Temple activities at Passover included family offerings, prayers, and participation in public teaching. Visitors, pilgrims, and teachers clustered in the shaded porticoes, gathering disciples and debating the Law. This was not youthful curiosity but a marker of destiny and vocation. - (aaron, 2010; Daneshmand, 2016). Finding Jesus so absorbed in these affairs that he lost track of his parents' journey home signals that his "business" was not ordinary business—it resonated with a singular sense of necessity.

Mary's question carries emotional weight. She and Joseph had traveled an entire day before discovering Jesus's absence, suffering mounting anxiety with each retraced step. Finding him in the temple, attentive to teachers and unfazed by parental distress, must have felt both bewildering and distressing. Jesus's response, *"Did you not know I must be in the things of my Father?"* as translated in a literal rendering, exposes the tension between his spiritual allegiance and his role as son within a human household. - (Daneshmand, 2016). Scholars clarify that the unusual phrasing in Greek invites debate among translators; some render it "in my Father's house," others, "about my Father's business." Both explanations seek to fill in the meaning supplied by the context of temple teaching and religious affairs.

Mary and Joseph's confusion records the ordinary limitations of human understanding when encountering divine purpose. Luke's Gospel notes that "they did not understand the saying," underscoring the mysterious quality of Jesus's self-awareness at such a young age. - (aaron, 2010). Yet, Luke's narrative balances revelation with humility. Though Jesus stands apart in claiming this special relationship, he returns home in obedience, submitting to the rhythms and expectations of family life. He resumes the pattern of respect, learning, and daily responsibility. His readiness to embrace ordinary duties while carrying extraordinary knowledge hints at a balance between obedience to God and honor towards human parents—a harmony of spiritual authority and humble submission. The story leaves echoes of gentle questions: How much did Jesus understand about his mission at twelve? To what extent did his family grasp the meaning of his words? In the interchange between Jesus and his parents, the Gospel writer draws readers into both the wonder of early revelation and the puzzle of growing divine wisdom revealed in the context of ordinary family life.

Three Interpretations of Jesus' Early Identity Claim and Theological Implications

The way Jesus calls God "my Father" in the Temple as a twelve-year-old continues to puzzle and inspire readers. Here, his awareness and words set up deep questions: how much did Jesus know about himself at this age, and how does this moment shed light on the unique blend of divine and human that he embodied, even in childhood? Three main ways of reading this story help clarify the different theological and historical questions at stake.

POSSIBILITY OF INTERPRETATION: 1:

Early Consciousness of Divine Sonship

One line of interpretation, the Early Consciousness of Divine Sonship, claims that **Jesus**, even at twelve, <u>fully understood his unique relationship with God</u> and the purpose of his life. Scholars in this camp point to his use of **"Father"**—not <u>"our Father"</u> as in public prayer, but "my Father"—which signals personal and immediate intimacy. Jesus' presence among the teachers hints at a confidence rooted in his identity. Many within evangelical scholarship argue this moment displays "an extraordinary self-awareness that lies behind his words." - (Schrock, n.d.). According to this view, Jesus combined knowledge far beyond his years with a sense of destiny; he knew why he came. Some describe this as an "identity not constructed" slowly, but revealed organically out of the unity of his personhood. - (Schrock, n.d.). Quoting this perspective, D. A. Carson writes, "Jesus was never less than the Son of God, and at every stage, he is presented… as uniquely in the Father's purposes." - (Schrock, n.d.). The heart of this interpretation sees the young Jesus not only as a precocious student but as a child living out an inborn calling, with identity and mission inseparable even at the threshold of adolescence.

POSSIBILITY OF INTERPRETATION 2:

Emerging Vocational Awareness

Another set of interpreters, favoring an Emerging Vocational Awareness, view Jesus as experiencing a genuine process of growth and learning, discovering more about his role over time. His words about being ***"about my Father's business"*** are seen as a public step into self-understanding rather than a final arrival at it. This reading draws attention to the narrative context—Jesus sits, questions, listens, and answers, still growing "in wisdom and stature" (**Luke 2:52**). Scholars such as Howard Marshall capture this idea, writing, "Jesus expresses an awakening recognition of his task, not its complete grasp." - (Schrock, n.d.). The moment in the Temple becomes a marker along the way, not the endpoint. Jesus' humanity finds expression in his openness to learn, question, and grow in his calling—a process that includes mystery and discovery. Evangelical writers supporting this approach stress Jesus' real childhood, reminding readers that "he increased in wisdom" meant actual change and development. - (Schrock, n.d.). The story therefore spotlights the maturing of vocation, with Jesus' sense of purpose expanding like the horizons of any growing child, yet with the difference that the center of this awareness is God as Father.

POSSIBILITY OF INTERPRETATION 3:

Symbolic Proclamation of Messianic Identity

Another way to read this story comes through the Symbolic Proclamation of Messianic Identity perspective. Here, the focus turns to how Luke shapes his Gospel. This approach sees Jesus' statement less as a record of inner psychological experience and more as a declaration for the Gospel's hearers and readers. Within this frame, Jesus' words announce his **identity** <u>as God's Son and Servant</u>, echoing Old Testament patterns. Luke sets the stage for Jesus as the one who fulfills and transcends the expectations of Adam, Israel, and David. - (Schrock, n.d.). Evangelicals embracing this narrative-centered reading claim "the child's confession is programmatic" for the Gospel, not necessarily a detailed window into Jesus' personal consciousness at twelve but a lens through which God's redemptive plan is made clear. - (Schrock, n.d.). The statement's main purpose becomes theological—showing readers that Jesus is God's agent and heir within the line of Jewish expectation, using a childhood episode as a means to reveal a much larger truth about divine action in history.

POSSIBILITY OF INTERPRETATION (Combined)

Theological Implications for Divine and Human Natures

Each of these interpretations involves questions about how **Jesus'** divinity and **humanity** fit together—especially when considering the young, growing Jesus. The Early Consciousness view leans toward a picture of Jesus as always aware of <u>his divine identity</u>. The Emerging Vocational Awareness see him as learning and discovering, capturing a genuine developmental process. The Symbolic Proclamation perspective places emphasis on what the story reveals for faith and teaching rather than for historical psychology. All three, though, must grapple with the reality of the Incarnation, when God became fully human and experienced time, learning, and growth within the world. The mystery at the core is what later theology calls the hypostatic union: Jesus, true God and true man, remaining one person. Evangelical theologians describe this as the heart of Christian faith, where "God's Son takes the form of a servant… born of woman, born under the law". - (Schrock, n.d.; *Jesus and the Identity of God*, n.d.). This tension shapes how Christians come to understand salvation: a mission planned from all eternity, yet enacted within the world of human limitation and growth. - (*Jesus and the Identity of God*, n.d.). The Temple story in Luke, then, serves as a window into how Jesus could both seek his Father with genuine youth and display a divine mission unclouded by accident.

Summary and Reflection of Chapter 7

Now that we have explored **Jesus's declaration at twelve years old**—*"I must be about my Father's business"*—within its rich Jewish context and considered the different ways scholars interpret his early self-awareness, we can better appreciate **how this moment shapes our understanding of his unique identity**. Whether seen as a clear sign of divine sonship, a growing sense of purpose, or a symbolic message for readers, Jesus's words invite us to reflect on the balance between human growth and divine mission. This story encourages us to embrace both the mystery and the meaning behind Jesus's life, inspiring deeper curiosity and thoughtful discussion as we continue to explore who he is and what his calling means for us today.

Reference List of Chapter 7:

Primary Biblical Reference:

Luke 2:49-50 The Rare 'Statement of a Child (**Jesus at 12**): *"I Must be about My Father's Business"* Mentioned in According to; the Bible – New King James Version.

Other References:

Daneshmand, J. (2016, September 22). *The Art of Translation: An Example from Luke 2.49*. - thetwocities.com

Jesus and the Identity of God. (n.d.). - Ntwrightpage.com.

Schrock, D. (n.d.). *Jesus as the Son of God*. - thegospelcoalition.org

aaron. (2010, November 4). *The Interpretation of Luke 2:49 and the Significance of the Temple in the Gospel of Luke*. - aarongiesler.com

Chapter 8:

Rare Case of…

Adolescence &

YOUTH of JESUS

A Compressed Record of '18-Years-of-Life' in One Verse

<u>Luke 2:52</u> "*Jesus grew in wisdom and in stature and in favor (grace) with God and all the people*". **According to; the Bible – New Living Translation.**

Reading Luke's One-Line-Resume of <u>Jesus' Growth</u>

Many readers of the Gospels find themselves puzzled by a striking gap: after the detailed stories of Jesus' birth and infancy, **his early life is summarized <u>in just one brief verse</u>.** Unlike the rich narratives about his later ministry, <u>the years **between** childhood and the start of his public work</u> remain <u>almost completely silent</u>. This absence raises questions about why such a significant **part of Jesus' life is left largely unexplored**, and what that silence might mean for how we understand him.

This chapter examines that single verse—**<u>Luke 2:52</u>**—and considers <u>the many reasons the Gospel writers might have chosen to keep Jesus' youth so compressed</u>. By exploring litcrary choices, theological intentions, and pastoral implications, it offers fresh perspectives on the significance of this narrative gap. Through analysis of different interpretive approaches, readers are invited to reflect on what Luke's brief summary reveals and what meanings lie in the quiet spaces of the story.

Analysis and Implications of <u>Luke 2:52</u> (explaining the literary and theological significance and providing interpretive guidance)

Gospel writers present Jesus' youth with deliberate brevity, offering only a single verse—**Luke 2:52**—<u>between the infancy narratives and the start of His public ministry</u>. Four distinct frameworks help explain this narrative choice, each bringing out unique values and doctrines within the Christian tradition.

Theological Focus on Public Ministry

The first interpretation sees the Gospel silence as a purposeful choice by the evangelists. They concentrate their storytelling on Jesus' redemptive mission, rather than His early years, to keep the focus on what the message of salvation demands. This phrase signals development and readiness without distracting from the central theme—the proclamation of God's salvation through Jesus, often referred to as the kerygma. - (Guzik, 2022; *Luke 2 - the Biblical Illustrator - Bible Commentaries - StudyLight.org*, 2025). **Luke 2:52** works as a literary hinge, providing just enough to assure readers of

Jesus' preparation: *"And Jesus grew in wisdom and stature, and in favor with God and man."*

Theological reasoning here draws from the evangelical conviction that **the Gospel's main intent is to proclaim the good news of Jesus' death and resurrection**. Because of this, narrative details about His youth could dilute or cloud that clear, saving message. Evangelical scholars—such as those cited in standard commentaries—regularly echo that the real meaning rests in Jesus' public acts and final sacrifice. Accepting this interpretation leads readers to focus their faith on Jesus' redeeming work and the core message, rather than treat the Gospels as full biographies.

Respect for Privacy and Humility

A second interpretation points toward respect for privacy and humility—both in the example Jesus set and in the way Gospel writers honored Him. This reading proposes that by leaving Jesus' daily growing years mostly untouched, Scripture affirms His real, humble participation in ordinary family and village life. The absence of extraordinary childhood stories supports evangelical ideas about **the incarnate Christ growing** *"in favor with God and man,"* much like any other Jewish boy. - (Guzik, 2022). Luke 2:52 gives a dignified summary, depicting a steady, healthy maturing without spectacle or supernatural display.

This approach highlights the humility of Jesus' incarnation. Far from presenting a sensational or triumphalist messianic figure from childhood, the <u>Gospels avoid overstating His early life</u>. Such restraint models Christlike **humility** to readers and counters ancient ideas of divine royalty entering history with fanfare. Evangelical commentators often link **Jesus' experience to common people**, showing that <u>He lived and grew as they did</u>, and this understanding encourages believers to value quiet faithfulness, not just public deeds. The theological impact shifts attention to how Jesus shares in the everyday human journey, inviting all people to see their own lives reflected in His own humanly natural life.

Lost or Unrecorded Traditions

A third explanation suggests that stories about Jesus' youth may have existed in early Christian communities but were never written down in the Gospels. Ancient traditions could have been shared or remembered orally, yet **the Gospel authors**, <u>through the Holy Spirit's guidance</u>, only included what offered spiritual benefit to their audiences. - (Guzik, 2022). Luke's single summary verse may signal that the writer knew of such material, or at least, the curiosity surrounding Jesus' boyhood.

For those who appreciate historical inquiry, this interpretation bridges curiosity with scriptural confidence. Evangelical doctrine often teaches that the canon of Scripture provides all that believers require for faith and life, while recognizing that not every historical detail gets preserved in the biblical record. The Gospels reflect careful selection, showing that inspiration guides not only what to include but also what to leave out. This helps readers rest their trust in the sufficiency of Scripture, rather than feel deficient for gaps in the record.

Emphasizing Jesus' Uniqueness through Silence

A final interpretation sees Gospel silence as a way of underscoring the unique nature of Jesus Himself. The absence of elaborate youth narratives sets Him apart from ordinary biographical subjects and from legendary heroes whose early exploits fill pages of ancient literature. In Jesus' case, the mystery drives readers to engage not with data alone, but to approach Him with reverence and spiritual openness.

This approach matches **evangelical Christology**, which underscores Jesus' <u>one-of-a-kind role as the Son of God</u>. The Gospel texts invite readers to encounter Him not only as a historical figure but as the living, divine Redeemer. - (*Luke 2 - the Biblical Illustrator - Bible*

Commentaries - StudyLight.org, 2025). The impact of this interpretation lies in encouraging faith: encountering Jesus fully through the witness of the Spirit and the biblical testimony, rather than seeking exhaustive explanation.

These four interpretations reveal the richness and thoughtful design of the Gospel narratives. They guide believers to see how even narrative silence shapes their understanding of Christ's preparation and character. Each approach prompts deeper reflection on what **Luke 2:52** chooses to declare, and, just as importantly, on what it leaves sacredly unspoken.

Explanations for Gospel Silence and Their Theological Impact (distinct possibly interpretive reasons and guidance on textual support and perspectives)

Narrative silence often prompts as many questions as overt statements. The brief mention of Jesus' youth in Luke 2:52 stands among the most discussed gaps in the Gospels. Why did the Gospel writers compress nearly two decades of Jesus' life into a single sentence? The silence is striking. Four major interpretive approaches help to explain this, each offering a unique perspective on what the brevity means for readers, both theologically and pastorally.

POSSIBILITY OF INTERPRETATION 1:

Theological Focus on Public Ministry

The first interpretation sees **the Gospels' silence** as <u>an intentional theological decision</u>. Rather than offering a biography of Jesus' complete life, <u>the Gospel writers chose to emphasize salvation history</u>. Their aim was not simply to provide interesting facts but to highlight the redemptive work that began with **Jesus' public ministry**. The Gospels frequently mark a shift from Jesus' hidden years to the time *"when Jesus began his ministry"* (**Luke 3:23**). The accounts focus on events that had redemptive weight—teachings, miracles, the cross, and the resurrection—while grouping the earlier years as preparatory. <u>**Luke 2:52** serves as a vital bridge</u>. It acknowledges that *"Jesus grew in <u>wisdom</u>, <u>stature</u>, and <u>favor with God</u> <u>and people</u>"*, tracing a line of preparation leading toward mission. - (*Luke 2:52 - Verse-By-Verse Bible Commentary - StudyLight.org*, 2025). Evangelical commentators often stress that the heart of the story is not the private, hidden years but what Jesus did to accomplish salvation. Donald C. Fleming points out that the Gospel's writers highlight "the need for him to know and do his Father's will," with public ministry revealing the Father's purpose most clearly. - (Fleming, 2005). Theologically, this interpretation underscores that salvation history takes center stage. The details left unreported reinforce what matters most: the saving work Christ came to do.

POSSIBILITY OF INTERPRETATION 2:

Respect for Privacy and Humility

A second approach interprets silence as respect for Jesus' humility and the **privacy of those formative years**. The understated narrative around Jesus' life before age thirty speaks to his willingness to participate in the ordinary rhythms of human existence. Jesus underwent the growth, learning, and waiting common to every human, but he did so without seeking recognition or acclaim during those years. Evangelical writers note that Jesus' hiddenness before public ministry expresses true humility, echoing the overarching Gospel theme that *"the Son of Man did not come to be served, but to serve"* - (**Mark 10:45**). By leaving most of his youth uncelebrated and "under the radar," Jesus models patience and alignment with God's timing. This approach keeps the focus off biographical curiosity and directs it toward the depth of Jesus' identification with ordinary people. Adam Clarke observes that trials and unknown seasons are "cheerfully supported...because in all they had Jesus with them; but now they are in distress and misery because he is behind in Jerusalem". - (Clarke, 1832). <u>This interpretation encourages readers to value what is hidden and ordinary</u>, recognizing that even unglamorous seasons may be filled with meaning.

POSSIBILITY OF INTERPRETATION 3:

Lost or Unrecorded Traditions

Another explanation rests on the limits of memory and tradition. Some scholars propose that oral traditions about Jesus' early life may have existed within the community but were never included in the Gospels or were lost over time. Luke's solitary summary in 2:52 could be read as a respectful nod to traditions the evangelist chose not to detail— either because they were external to his sources or because he could not verify them. This perspective helps explain **Luke's careful statement** that *he "investigated everything from the beginning"* (**Luke 1:3**), suggesting the possibility of selecting only <u>what serves the community's faith</u>. Evangelical perspectives on Gospel formation often remind readers that the Gospels are not exhaustive records but inspired witnesses to essential truths. - (Green, 2018). This interpretation frames the gap as an invitation to humility—accepting mystery instead of historical completeness and **trusting in what was revealed** <u>as spiritually necessary</u>.

POSSIBILITY OF INTERPRETATION 4:

Emphasizing Jesus' Uniqueness through Silence

A final interpretive lens contends that silence about Jesus' early years actually marks him as unique among ancient figures. Biographies from antiquity often offer detailed accounts of their subject's youth, showing early genius or giving biographical clues to explain greatness. By contrast, the Gospels' silence invites readers to know Jesus on divine rather than merely human terms. His uniqueness as the Son of God is not rooted in a traceable psychology or in the exploits of youth but instead in identity and calling. This approach draws from the Gospel writers' practice of presenting Jesus' authority as rooted in his relationship with the Father, not in traditional biography. Quoting evangelical commentary, in the Gospel of Luke; 12-years-old boy Jesus "reminded his parents of his unique relationship with his heavenly Father". - (Fleming, 2005). Theologically, this urges readers to interpret Jesus' development through a spiritual lens, affirming Christ's uniqueness and the mystery shrouding his incarnate life. - (*Luke Commentaries & Sermons | Precept Austin*, 2018). The absence of a conventional narrative lets Jesus stand apart as **the Incarnate Word** <u>whose purpose outpaces normal life</u> stories.

These interpretive frameworks do not compete so much as they offer complementary windows, each calling readers deeper into the scriptural portrait of Jesus—the Savior whose life, even in silence, speaks with care and intention.

Summary and Reflection of Chapter 8

Now that we have explored the various reasons behind the Gospel's brief mention of <u>Jesus' youth in **Luke 2:52**</u>, we can appreciate how this narrative choice invites us to focus on **His growth, humility**, and unique mission <u>without distraction from unnecessary detail</u>. Understanding the theological purpose, respect for Jesus' ordinary life, possible lost traditions, and the emphasis on His divine identity helps us approach these silent years with thoughtful reflection rather than unanswered curiosity. This insight encourages readers and study leaders alike <u>to embrace the mystery as part of faith</u>, deepening our appreciation for Jesus' preparation and calling us to engage more fully with the transformative message of His public ministry and redemptive work.

Reference List of Chapter 8

Primary Biblical Reference:

Luke 2:52 "*Jesus grew* in **wisdom** and in **stature** and in <u>*favor with God and all the people*</u>". **According to; the Bible – New Living Translation.**

Other References:

Guzik, D. (2022, June 16). *Study Guide for Luke 2*. - BlueLetterBible.org

Luke 2 - The Biblical Illustrator - Bible Commentaries - StudyLight.org. (2025). - StudyLight.org

Luke Commentaries & Sermons | Precept Austin. (2018). - Preceptaustin.org.

Luke 2:52 - Verse-by-Verse Bible Commentary - StudyLight.org. (2025). - StudyLight.org.

Chapter 9:

Rare case of…

An Unusual PROPHET

John the Baptist's Ministry, Diet, Style, and Elijah Echoes

Matthew 3:1-6 According to; the Bible – English Standard Version.

A Man with a Life of Singularity

Imagine a **solitary figure** standing at the edge of a barren wilderness, his rough garment catching the dry breeze, calling out to crowds who have journeyed far from their homes and daily routines. His voice cuts through the stillness **with an urgent message**, stirring hearts toward change not just in behavior but deep within the soul. This man's presence is both unsettling and captivating—a living reminder of ancient promises and expectations long held by a people hungry for renewal. **His lifestyle**, simple yet striking, marks him as different from the religious leaders and rulers of his day, setting him apart in a way that invites reflection on what it truly means to prepare for something momentous. **The image of this wild prophet** challenges us to reconsider familiar stories and invites deeper inquiry into his unique place within a larger unfolding narrative.

John's Ministry and Prophetic Persona (Matthew 3:1–6)

John the Baptist emerges in **Matthew 3:1–6** as a figure whose message and manner echo some of the deepest traditions of Hebrew prophecy. His central proclamation—*"**Repent, for the kingdom of**"* *heaven **has come near***"—struck at the heart of Israel's longing for deliverance and renewal. <u>**Repentance**</u>, in John's teaching, <u>demanded more than sorrow for past wrongdoing</u> or outward religious performance. **It required an inward transformation**, a <u>complete change of will and direction</u>. This was **an urgent summons to prepare for <u>God's arrival and a new work</u>**. John's message called individuals and communities to turn from the patterns of sin and complacency that had gathered during centuries without prophetic leadership. As <u>prophecy had fallen **silent** since Malachi</u>, John's ministry arrived as the first true prophetic voice in **<u>over four hundred years</u>**, awakening expectation and signaling the nearness of Messianic promise. - (*Matthew 03.01*, 2025; *Matthew 3:1 - Verse-By-Verse Bible Commentary - StudyLight.org*, 2025). For Jewish listeners, many of whom ached for a renewed encounter with God amid Roman rule and religious stagnation, **John the Baptist's call <u>evoked</u> the sense of <u>a long-awaited turning point</u>**.

The physical context of **John's ministry** only heightened its spiritual weight. He preached not in the bustling streets of Jerusalem or the courts of the temple, but **<u>in the wilderness</u>** of Judea. **This wilderness**, a strip of landscape lying west of the Dead Sea, <u>carried rich biblical symbolism</u>. It recalled the wanderings of Israel before entering the promised land and the solitary **places that prophets like Elijah and Moses frequented** when <u>seeking encounter with God</u>. The wilderness, with its open expanse and lack of human comfort, offered a space for powerful spiritual encounter and renewal. John's choice to preach there served to separate his message from the religious establishment—his voice was heard far from the centers of institutional influence, away from the rituals and regulations that many had come to associate with holiness. - (*Matthew 03.01*, 2025; *Matthew 3:1 - Verse-By-Verse Bible Commentary - StudyLight.org*, 2025). In this setting, the people who came to John were led, both literally and spiritually, into a place of vulnerability, reflection, and openness to divine transformation.

John's outward appearance and daily practices <u>reinforced his prophetic identity</u>. Matthew describes him dressed in a garment of camel's hair with a leather belt around his waist, subsisting on locusts and wild honey. **This description** mirrors that of Elijah in **<u>2 Kings 1:8</u>**, where he is called *"a man with a garment of hair and a leather belt about his waist."* The connection was unmistakable for John's hearers. Such attire and diet marked John as a man set apart, uninterested in the comforts or fashions of his day. His rough clothing and simple food spoke of self-denial, a sober and focused life, and a disdain for the excess and luxury found in religious and social elites. This lifestyle was not mere eccentricity—by rejecting worldly pleasures and status, John modeled the seriousness of his message and embodied the transformation he demanded from others. - (*Matthew 03.01*, 2025). His example suggested that those who prepare the way for God's kingdom must themselves stand free from the distractions and corruptions of society. For onlookers, this presentation offered both a challenge and an invitation, as it contrasted sharply with the ornate robes of temple priests and the plenty of life in Jerusalem.

Underlying **John's ministry** was a much older expectation: <u>the return of **Elijah** before the arrival of the Messiah</u>. **Malachi 4:5** prophesied that Elijah would come as a forerunner, and by John's dress, actions, and message, he strongly resembled that ancient prophet. <u>Jesus even identifies John as *"the Elijah who was to come"*</u> in **Matthew 11:14**, confirming the link that many would have seen instinctively. This connection did more than situate John in the prophetic tradition—it marked the moment as <u>a bridge between the old promises and the new reality</u> of the Messiah's arrival. **John the Baptist's ministry** <u>opened a new chapter in salvation history</u>, inviting Israel to wake from spiritual sleep and expect something entirely new. - (*Matthew 03.01*, 2025; *Matthew 3:1 - Verse-By-Verse Bible Commentary - StudyLight.org*, 2025). John was more than a prophet just warning of judgment or crying for reform; he had a singular task to prepare people for the very presence of God among them.

John's prophetic persona draws deeply from Israel's memory, yet it also reshapes expectation for what a messenger of God might be. His life and message challenge easy religious assumptions and demand a response. The ways his identity and legacy have been understood continues to invite debate and wonder among readers and communities who seek to grasp the full measure of his role in the unfolding story of the Messiah.

José E. Espinoza

Interpretations of <u>John the Baptist's Role</u> and <u>Influence on Jesus' Early Ministry</u>

POSSIBILITY OF INTERPRETATION 1:

John as the Forerunner Preparing the Way

Many Christians look to John the Baptist as the forerunner who prepared the people for the arrival of Jesus. John's entire ministry revolved around making *"ready the way of the Lord"* (**Isaiah 40:3**). He took up this calling through preaching repentance and baptizing everyone willing to respond, urging them to turn their lives around and anticipate the Messiah's appearance. **By calling people to confess their sins** and submit to a baptism of repentance in the Jordan River, John offered a sign that cleansing was necessary before entering into God's renewed covenant (**Matt 3:2–6**). The wilderness setting, where his message first sounded, symbolized new beginnings, much like Israel's formative time after the exodus. Instead of hiding from society, John went there to inaugurate a spiritual transformation, drawing crowds who came curious or desperate for hope. His baptisms did not create some new ritual but drew from established practices of

<u>washing for purification</u> - (Lev 11). In a world where many felt spiritually stagnant, John's ministry cleared a spiritual pathway, setting people's hearts to expect and recognize Jesus—a foundation upon which Christ would soon build with a message of forgiveness and a new covenant relationship. - (Burnett, 2015; *John the Baptist - Search Results Provided by BiblicalTraining*, 2025).

POSSIBILITY OF INTERPRETATION 2:

John as a Symbolic Elijah Figure

Looking more deeply, another way to understand John's role draws from his clear identification with Elijah, one of Israel's most iconic prophets. People living in John's time already expected Elijah's return as a sign of coming restoration and judgment (**Malachi 3:1, 4:5**). **John <u>dressed, lived, and spoke like</u> Elijah,** with camel's hair clothing and a wild lifestyle in the desert, echoing the experiences of the Old Testament prophet fleeing to the wilderness (**1 Kings 19:4**). This public appearance called to mind old prophecies, giving hope that God would revive true faith in their generation. Yet it also raised the stakes, since Elijah's ministry involved confronting false religion and warning of God's judgment. John's message of repentance to all, including Pharisees and political leaders, was an urgent call for genuine covenant loyalty—not just inherited privilege (**Luke 3:7–9**). When **Jesus described John** as a prophet and **more than a prophet** (**Matt 11:9–15**), he affirmed John as a fulfillment of Malachi's words about a messenger who would prepare the way before the Lord. This highlights how John's ministry restored the bold, challenging, and redemptive authority of prophets before the silence between the testaments, bridging the old and new through a charge to return to wholehearted worship of God. - (*John the Baptist - Search Results Provided by; BiblicalTraining*, 2025; Burnett, 2015).

POSSIBILITY OF INTERPRETATION 3:

John as an Eschatological Prophet

A third interpretation presents John as an **eschatological prophet**, meaning he announced the arrival of God's decisive, world-changing act. Many recognized John's message as apocalyptic, full of urgency and anticipation. He warned that **the Messiah would gather the fruitful into the kingdom** and cast the unrepentant aside like chaff into fire. **The baptism John offered**; was not only about washing away past wrong doings but marking readiness for the moment when everything would change. This approach points to John's understanding of time: **the old order was ending**, and God was about to intervene powerfully through His chosen one (**Matt 3:10-12**). John's proclamation drew from the tradition of Old Testament prophets, but he pressed the people to respond without delay, *"for the kingdom of heaven is near."* Interpreting John as an **eschatological** figure helps explain his fierce tone, uncompromising call for new obedience, and the sense that with Jesus behind him, history itself was changing. - (Burnett, 2015). His radical message fit within broader Jewish longing for deliverance and renewal, but he surprised many by placing the emphasis on repentance and spiritual fruit, not political liberation.

POSSIBILITY OF INTERPRETATION 4:

John's Influence on Jesus' Early Ministry

Examining the **relationship between John and Jesus** adds a fourth lens, highlighting John's pivotal influence on Jesus' early ministry. **When Jesus chose to be baptized by John**, it indicated a public recognition of John's prophetic status and submission to God's unfolding plan. **This moment marked both** a passing of the torch and a declaration of continuity between their missions. John's ministry, bold enough to rebuke even royalty, set the stage for Jesus' own confrontations with spiritual and political authorities (**Luke 3:19–20**).

While John came to prepare a people ready for the Messiah, Jesus arrived to fulfill what John's preaching pointed towards—a new age marked not only by forgiveness of sins, but the indwelling of God's Spirit. The connection between their ministries reveals points of deep similarity in calls for repentance, yet divergence in the fullness of the salvation Jesus brought—a difference Jesus himself explained when he said, *"among those born of women **there is no one greater than John**; yet the one who is least in the kingdom of God is greater than he"*. - (**Luke 7:28**; *John the Baptist - Search Results Provided by BiblicalTraining*, 2025; Burnett, 2015). Each interpretive framework adds a piece to a fuller picture of John's role in salvation history, tracing how his witness shaped the very foundation of Christian faith.

Summary and Reflection of Chapter 9

Understanding **John the Baptist's unique role** as <u>a prophetic forerunner</u> **who** calls for true repentance and **prepares the way for Jesus** invites us to reflect more deeply on our own readiness for transformation. His **wilderness ministry**, **austere lifestyle**, and powerful message challenge us to move beyond superficial faith and embrace an <u>inward change that aligns with God's kingdom</u>. Now that we have explored the layers of John's identity—as Elijah's return, **an eschatological herald**, and <u>a key figure shaping Jesus' early mission</u>—we can approach his story not just as history but as a living call to live with urgency and openness to God's work in the world. This understanding equips young believers, educators, and seekers alike to engage meaningfully with the Gospel message and inspire thoughtful conversation about how we, too, might prepare the way for renewed faith today.

Reference List for Chapter 9

Primarily Biblical Reference:

Matthew 3:1-6 Rare Case of a '**Prophet**'/'**Messenger**' **Such as John the Baptist**; Mentioned According to; the Bible – English Standard Version + other Versions

Other References:

Burnett, D. C. (2015, February 19). *Eschatological Prophet of Restoration: Luke's Theological Portrait of John the Baptist in Luke 3:1-6*. - academia.edu.

John the Baptist - Search results provided by BiblicalTraining. (2025). - biblicaltraining.org.

Matthew 03.01. (2025). @Logos. – logos.com

Matthew 3:1 - Verse-by-Verse Bible Commentary - StudyLight.org. (2025). - studylight.org.

Chapter 10:

Rare Case of...

JESUS Being BAPTIZED

Why Jesus Submitted Himself to a Baptism for Sinners

<u>Matthew 3:13-15</u> According to; (the Bible) – New Living Translation

José E. Espinoza

Ritual, Identification, or Example?

Why would **Jesus**, <u>who was without sin</u>, choose to undergo a <u>baptism meant for those (sinners) seeking repentance</u>? What does it mean for the Son of God to step into the waters alongside ordinary people preparing for a new life? Could this act be a simple ritual, or is it something deeper—a statement about **identity**, **mission**, and **obedience**? These questions invite us to look closely at a moment that puzzles many readers but holds rich meaning beneath the surface. Exploring why Jesus submitted to baptism challenges us to rethink assumptions and consider how this singular event connects to the broader story of faith and following God's call. Through reflection on this scene, we step into a conversation that has engaged believers across centuries, revealing layers of purpose that continue to speak today.

Narrative Analysis: John's Hesitation (or Resistance to baptize Jesus), Jesus' Reason, Public Identification, and Theophany (Informational)

The moment Jesus entered the waters of the Jordan and submitted to John's baptism, He sparked wide-ranging debate among Christians, pastors, and theologians. Why would the sinless Son of God accept a ritual associated with repentance? Three major theological models—ritual cleansing or ministry initiation, identification with humanity, and demonstration as an **example** for believers—open doors to a deeper understanding of this cryptic scene in Matthew.

Jesus' baptism is sometimes understood as a ritual act of dedication—an inauguration marking His public entrance into God's service. **In Old Testament tradition**, prophets and priests often went through rites of purification or consecration before beginning a divine mission. Isaiah described his own calling in the temple as an act of cleansing: *"Your guilt is taken away and your sin atoned for"* (**Isaiah 6:7**). Priests would be washed and anointed before ministering at the altar (**Leviticus 8**). In this light, **Jesus' baptism is not about repenting of sin**, but **about signaling a formal dedication and transition** into messianic ministry. The New Testament often links baptism to the launching of a new life or calling. *"We must carry out all that God requires,"* Jesus says in **Matthew 3:15.** - (Lainey, 2024), capturing the necessity of His obedience—not for His own repentance, but <u>to inaugurate God's plan in a new way</u>. At the same moment, the descent of the Spirit marks Him out and the voice from heaven establishes His identity as the Beloved Son. - (*Commentary on Matthew 3:13-17*, 2011). The public nature of Jesus' baptism echoes times when leaders were called and set aside before the whole community.

A second, equally compelling explanation unfolds as Jesus stands in line with the many ordinary people waiting for John's baptism. Here, the emphasis shifts from ritual cleansing to identification with the broken and burdened. **Jesus**, who had no sin of His own, <u>chose to stand shoulder to shoulder with those longing for forgiveness</u>. His willingness to be counted among sinners foreshadows the very heart of His earthly mission: <u>standing in solidarity with the lost, the outcast, and the guilty</u>. The act of joining sinners in the Jordan was a preview of His later willingness to touch lepers, dine with tax collectors, and defend the woman caught in adultery. **By submitting to baptism**, <u>Jesus displays a humility and empathy that would become the hallmark of His ministry</u>. His identification here is personal and costly—He "carried the weight of our sins on his shoulders" in baptism, just as He would on the cross. - (Lainey, 2024). Paul later writes, *"God made him who had no sin to be sin for us"* (**2 Corinthians 5:21**), a verse that draws directly from this sense of profound identification. Instead of standing apart, Jesus dives into the current of human brokenness, affirming the dignity of the lowly and the love for the rejected.

The third approach focuses on **Jesus as the pioneer** <u>who shows the way of obedience to those who would follow</u>. By submitting to baptism, Jesus lays down <u>a pattern for discipleship</u>, making clear that baptism is not optional or arbitrary, but a central act of allegiance for anyone who claims to walk with God. His words to John—"it is proper for us in this way to fulfill all righteousness" (**Matthew 3:15**)—become a template for generations of believers. Early Christians saw baptism as initiation into the new community, a dying and rising with Christ marked by water (**Romans 6:4**). Jesus' practice gives legitimacy and meaning to this rite. **It is not just symbolic**, but <u>an act that weaves each follower into His own story of obedience</u>, death, and resurrection. Through baptism, Christians publicly declare their identity and pledge to walk according to the pattern He set.

Many scholars and pastors recognize all three interpretations working together like harmonic notes in a chord. The Gospel text's richness supports an approach that refuses to flatten Jesus' baptism into any single explanation. Instead, the event serves several functions at once: commissioning Jesus for service, expressing His solidarity with humanity, and setting an example for His disciples. This combination supports the biblical narrative, with its layers of meaning and moments of resonance across different places in Scripture. - (*Commentary on Matthew 3:13-17*, 2011). When these interpretations are woven together, they offer **a portrait of Jesus'** baptism that is both **<u>mysterious</u> and <u>beautiful</u>**.

Each of **these meanings** can shape a Christian's understanding of their own baptism—a moment of cleansing, solidarity, and commitment. Standing in the river, embraced by the voice of God the Father declaring Him as beloved Son, and the visual phenomenon of the Holy Spirit ascending upon Him like a dove, Jesus emerges set apart and affirmed by God. The mystery and clarity found in His baptism continue to invite believers into a living faith, formed by water, Spirit, and radical obedience. - (Lainey, 2024; *Commentary on Matthew 3:13-17*, 2011). The story leaves Him poised on the edge of a new path, ready for the testing, teaching, and sacrifice that define His messianic mission.

Interpretive Evaluation: Ritual, Solidarity, Example, and a Multifaceted Understanding (Informational)

POSSIBILITY OF INTERPRETATION 1

Ritual Cleansing and Initiation into Ministry

Jesus standing in the waters of the Jordan has often been understood as a moment of ritual transition. Many evangelical thinkers point to the baptism as the public inauguration of his earthly ministry. In this view, **the act was not about Jesus repenting of sin**; it carried the meaning of dedication and consecration, much like ceremonies that inaugurated prophets or priests in ancient Israel. Old Testament patterns highlight how priests were washed, anointed, and commissioned for God's work (see **Exodus 29; Leviticus 8**). Stepping into the water, **Jesus was not acknowledging guilt**, but crossing the sacred boundary from private life into his calling as Messiah.

John's role as the forerunner echoed the Old Testament tradition, **preparing the way** by calling people to repentance and readiness **for the coming kingdom**. Jesus, by stepping into John's baptism, publicly identified his mission and embraced this divine commissioning. Aquinas draws out this theme, declaring that "it was necessary for Christ to be baptized by John, in order that He might **sanctify baptism**" and so his baptism made the rite (or sacred ritual later) <u>holy for those who would follow.</u> - (Nyarko, 2024). Consistent with this, the act of baptism marked a sacred threshold; here the Father's voice announced Christ's identity and the Holy Spirit descended, anointing him for public work (**Luke 3:21–22**). Early Christian writers saw this as Jesus aligning with the great figures of Israel's story—prophets, priests, and kings who began their service with ritual acts of dedication. - (*Baptism - Search Results Provided by BiblicalTraining*, 2025). Baptism, in this reading, was the beginning of Christ's open, messianic work—an event that brought divine affirmation and authority to his mission.

POSSIBILITY OF INTERPRETATION 2:

Identification with Humanity and Sinful People

Other interpreters look past ritual alone, focusing instead on Jesus' choice to stand with fallen people. **The New Testament insists that Jesus was without sin**, yet he submits to a baptism meant for repentance. **<u>This enigma</u>** has drawn many evangelical scholars to see in Jesus' act a powerful gesture of solidarity with humanity. Justin Martyr explained that Jesus "did not go to the river because He stood in need of baptism, … but because of the human race, which from Adam had fallen under the power of death and the guile of the serpent". - (Nyarko, 2024).

By undergoing baptism, Jesus took his place among those he came to save. He stands in the long line with tax collectors, soldiers, and common people—allowing himself to be counted among sinners, affirming both their need for repentance and his mission to rescue. Young (1995) emphasizes this theme, noting, "In His identity with the totality of human need, He submitted to baptism in order to affirm the process of redemption which was in action as a result of John's prophetic career". - (Nyarko, 2024). **This act of radical humility** shows not only God's compassion, but the foreshadowing of the cross. As Green (1988) observes, Jesus' baptism pointed ahead to his death: **"Jesus' cross became His baptism**, making the justification of the ungodly possible by dealing with the sins of the world". - (Nyarko, 2024). In this reading, the watery descent was a sign of the depths to which Jesus would go—down into human brokenness, up into resurrection life.

POSSIBILITY OF INTERPRETATION 3:

Demonstration as an Example to Followers

A third approach understands **Jesus' baptism as a deliberate act of example**. By entering the waters, Jesus shows his followers how to obey God and commit to kingdom living. Many evangelicals see this act as setting a pattern for all believers—a visible demonstration of humble submission that authenticates the practice of baptism in the church.

Aquinas wrote that **Christ's baptism was "necessary**…that He might sanctify baptism". - (Nyarko, 2024), tying this act to all future believers. Wilkins (2004) comments that Jesus "established a public link and continuity between John's message and His ministry and…endorsed the rite of baptism among Christians of all generations" - (Nyarko, 2024). In submitting to a rite he did not need, **Jesus told his disciples**: "Follow me, not just in words but in actions." This theme appears throughout the New Testament, where Christ's followers are told to imitate his humility and obedience (**Philippians 2; & 1 Peter 2:21**). The act demonstrates a baseline for Christian practice—one of surrender, repentance, and new beginning.

Holding these Interpretive Meanings Together

Evangelical teaching rarely stops at just one explanation. Many writers encourage readers to see these interpretations as complementary rather than competing. Jesus' baptism acts as **initiation**, **identification**, **anointing**, **and** **example**, all present in a single event. When the New Testament reflects on baptism, it draws out layers of meaning—ritual entry, sharing in Christ's death and resurrection, and the call to discipleship. - (Romans 6:3–4; Colossians 2:12, cited in *Baptism - Search Results Provided by BiblicalTraining*, 2025). Holding these views together allows the richness of the event to shape Christian life today: a beginning, a deep solidarity, a call to follow, and a sign of God's love moving into the world. - (Nyarko, 2024; *Baptism - Search Results Provided by BiblicalTraining*, 2025).

Summary and Reflection of Chapter 10

Now that we understand the rich and layered meaning behind **Jesus' baptism**—his dedication to God's mission, his deep identification with humanity, and his example of humble obedience—we can see how this event invites us into a fuller experience of faith. **It challenges us** to step into our own callings with commitment, to stand alongside others in their struggles with compassion, and to follow Jesus' path of obedience with confidence. Recognizing the baptism of Jesus as both a beginning and a promise; empowers believers to embrace this obedience to the baptism not just as a ritual, but as a living expression of identity and mission, preparing us to receive the Spirit's guidance as we journey forward in our own stories of faith.

Reference List of Chapter 10:

Primary Biblical Reference:

<u>Matthew 3;13-15</u> The Rare case of (why?) Jesus Christ should be Baptized (as a requirement in Jesus' mind), and John the Baptist experiencing conflict to accept it. Mentioned According to; the Bible – New Living Translation.

Other References:

Baptism - Search results provided by BiblicalTraining. (2025). - biblicaltraining.org
Commentary on Matthew 3:13-17. (2011, January 9). Working Preacher from Luther Seminary. – workingpreacher.org

Lainey. (2024, March 3). *Understanding Matthew 3:13-15: Why Jesus Chose Baptism.* - lemon8-app.com

Nyarko, E. (2024, July 6). *Understanding the Christian Sacrament of Baptism: Perspectives of Some New Testament Personalities.* European Journal of Theology and Philosophy. - doi.org

PART 4:

RARE CASES OF...

NEW MINISTRY

In The New Testament with Possibilities of Interpretation;

Chapter 11:

Rare Case of...

Temptation 'PARADOX' of Jesus

Jesus Tempted by Satan, yet Led by the Spirit to be Tempted

Matthew 4:1 … "***Jesus was led by the Spirit*** *into the wilderness **to be tempted** by the devil.* (Bible) – NIV

José E. Espinoza

Purpose and <u>Paradox</u> of the <u>Temptation</u> Journey

"Why would the Spirit lead Jesus into the wilderness, a place known for emptiness and danger, where temptation waits at every turn?" This question might come to mind when reading about Jesus' journey into the desert. It feels puzzling, **almost contradictory**—how can <u>the same Spirit that guides and protects also bring someone into such a harsh trial</u>? Imagine stepping away from everything familiar, into a lonely, challenging place, not by accident but in deliberate obedience. **The wilderness is more than a physical location**; it carries the weight of Israel's history filled with struggle, testing, and moments of both faithfulness and failure.

Many find themselves wondering why difficult times seem to come on their path, especially when they seek to follow God closely. Is hardship a sign of God's absence or punishment? Or could it be something deeper—an experience meant to reveal what lies beneath the surface of faith and character? This tension between divine care and human struggle lies at the heart of Jesus' time in the wilderness. **It calls us to wrestle with the reality** that <u>sometimes the Spirit's leading involves walking through challenges</u>, not around them.

For those wanting to understand this moment better—whether as personal encouragement or as material for teaching—it raises

148   *In The New Testament with Possibilities of Interpretation;*

important questions: **What does this paradox say about God's nature**? How does facing temptation shape readiness for the work ahead? And what might this story teach about spiritual strength coming through dependence on Scripture and trust rather than self-reliance? These are not easy questions, but they open the door to fresh ways of seeing how God's presence works even in the midst of hardship.

Such **reflections** invite readers <u>to consider their own experiences with struggle and guidance</u>. When life leads into difficult places, might there be purpose hidden beyond immediate discomfort? This introduction to the chapter sets the stage for exploring these tensions carefully, helping readers approach one of the Gospel's most mysterious episodes with curiosity and thoughtful attention.

Context, Paradox, Narrative Function, and Pastoral Significance of the Spirit-Led Temptation

"Then Jesus was led by the Spirit into the wilderness to be tempted by the devil." With this single verse, Matthew throws us into one of the Gospel's **most mysterious moments**. - (O'Donnell, n.d.; *Matthew*, 2025). Readers are left with a question: <u>**Why would the Holy Spirit**, the very presence of God, guide Jesus into a setting where temptation and confrontation with evil are guaranteed</u>? The wilderness here isn't

just an empty stretch of land. It echoes the long stretch of sand and silence that shaped Israel's story—a place marked by absence, lack, hunger, and exposure. Far from the comfort of community, Jesus steps into a landscape that tested his ancestors for forty years, exposing trust and doubt, faithfulness and failure.

The mention of "wilderness" brings up more than a memory of Israel's wanderings; it is a setting dense with meaning. For ancient Israel, the wilderness saw both God's mighty acts and their repeated failures. God provided manna and water, yet people grumbled and tested God at places like Meribah (Exodus 17:7). The Israelites lived day by day on God's provision, but discontent and disobedience kept resurfacing. Their tests were not just about passing or failing; they revealed the heart's condition and readiness for God's promises. - (O'Donnell, n.d.). By drawing the same setting around Jesus, Matthew wants readers to see continuity—a new "testing" with echoes of an old one. Jesus walks a path that Israel walked first, yet while Israel stumbled, Jesus faces what comes alone and unshielded.

When Matthew says Jesus was **"led by the Spirit,"** he focuses on the origin of this moment. There is no hint that Jesus wandered there by accident or stumbled into some snare. This direct language signals both **intent and trust**. The Spirit's leading is deliberate. This challenges every simple view that equates God's guidance with only pleasant, easy roads. Instead, divine initiative sometimes means embracing difficulty on purpose. The Spirit's involvement raises the stakes: Temptation is not just random trouble, nor evidence of divine neglect. God remains fully present, even when the path winds into struggle.

That sets up the <u>paradox</u>. If the Spirit is the one who draws Jesus to this lonely, difficult place, what does that say about the nature of God's goodness? Why allow a confrontation with evil instead of shielding the beloved Son? The question presses hard on our assumptions. Too often, trials are seen as interruptions or punishments, but this story pushes back. **The temptation in the wilderness isn't a trap or abandonment**. <u>It's a sacred space where purpose runs deeper than surface comfort</u>. God's leading does not always feel safe or gentle; sometimes it means exposure to the real hardship and choice. The purpose here is not harm but formation—a process where trust, faith, and spiritual clarity come to the surface right where pressure is greatest.

In **Matthew's Gospel**, the <u>wilderness testing acts as a major turning point</u>. It comes after Jesus' baptism, when the voice from heaven announces him as the beloved Son. Before Jesus preaches, heals, or calls disciples, he must face what the desert uncovers. This shows that **spiritual readiness does not depend on avoiding trouble**; <u>it grows by moving through it</u>. Temptation confronts Jesus not in a moment of weakness, but at the height of affirmation and commission. **By facing the devil's testing**, <u>Jesus reveals strength that emerges from obedience</u>, not from comfort or isolation. Had Jesus refused this leading, or if the Spirit had skipped over the hard place, ministry to others would lack substance. Unpreparedness could have meant a shallow message or a ministry that crumbles under pressure.

During this encounter, Jesus leans on Scripture rather than personal power. Each challenge from the devil meets a response rooted in words remembered and trusted. The episode also signals that God's power does not vanish in hardship. Instead, the Spirit's presence means Jesus faces temptation not as a victim, but as someone acting with divine endorsement and strength. - (*Matthew*, 2025; O'Donnell, n.d.). This detail serves as a guide for readers. Facing trials often strips away every resource except God's promises.

For anyone who wonders about the meaning of their own hardships, the wilderness story holds hope. Experiences that look like abandonment or unnecessary struggle could become places where faith deepens and God's guidance remains present, even behind the scenes. Divine sovereignty and human struggle stand together. **Trials do not prove God's absence**; <u>sometimes they mark where God is working most.</u>

This paradox, where <u>The Spirit leads toward struggle</u> instead of away, deserves closer exploration. The way it sheds light or confusion points to deeper purposes—ones that will need careful attention from several different angles.

Three Interpretive Views of Divine Testing and a Theological Synthesis

Divine testing in the life of Jesus opens up wide questions about God's purpose in bringing His Son, through the Holy Spirit, straight into temptation's path. Together, these offer a richer understanding of not only what Jesus faced, but also how God engages with His people in moments of trial. - (Koffa & Seminary, 2025) Christians through the centuries have drawn meaning from this mystery, developing three different interpretive frameworks.

POSSIBILITY OF INTERPRETATION 1:

Purification and Moral Formation

One rich interpretive lens is the view of purification and moral formation. This framework sees the Spirit's choice to lead Jesus into the wilderness as a process of moral proving, where holy character stands revealed and confirmed. This isn't about Jesus moving from imperfection to greater purity; rather, it is about His true, unstained obedience being tested openly. In this understanding, the wilderness becomes a spiritual crucible—like gold passed through fire or a vessel shaped on the potter's wheel—revealing the reality of holiness by meeting genuine opposition. The Hebrew Scriptures are filled with images of God using hardship as a place where His people are refined (Psalm 66:10; Malachi 3:3). Evangelical theologians such as Dietrich Bonhoeffer and John Stott emphasize that sanctification unfolds not in comfort but under pressure, with the presence of temptation exposing what is real in a person's walk with God. The Spirit's presence is not just comfort; His leading into the wild affirms divine intention: to demonstrate that holiness can endure in the presence of evil. - (Koffa & Seminary, 2025). For believers, this framework reassures that temptations themselves are not evidence of failure or abandonment. Rather, when the Spirit puts one in trying circumstances, He uses them to reveal spiritual reality, deepen trust, and shape character. The believer's ongoing surrender, daily asking the Spirit to search and form their heart, mirrors this process of sanctification.

POSSIBILITY OF INTERPRETATION 2:

Preparation for Public Ministry

A second interpretive focus is **preparation for ministry**. Here, the Spirit's leading of Jesus comes across as a form of divine training ground. Jesus, before any public teaching, healing, or miracle, first faces the testing in the desert. This preparation serves as a private rehearsal for the pressures of public ministry. Scriptural parallels abound—Moses' forty years as a shepherd, David's struggles before kingship, Paul's years in Arabia—all faced times of solitude and trial that prepared them for the tasks ahead. The Spirit does not tempt, but He positions Jesus in a place where He must cling to the Father's word, resist shortcuts for power, and choose faithfulness even when unseen (Matthew 4:1–11). Biblical scholars such as N.T. Wright and Craig Keener describe this as God's way of forming resilience and focus. In wilderness tests, hidden battles today become strength and integrity for tomorrow's calling. When one feels isolated or under spiritual attack, the Spirit might be forging qualities needed for mission and ministry yet to come (Koffa & Seminary, 2025). This framework encourages believers to see present trials not only as moral battles, but also as seasons God uses to equip, refine gifts, and clarify purpose for future service.

POSSIBILITY OF INTERPRETATION 3:

Conflict and Victory over Evil

A third influential perspective centers on **cosmic conflict**. Here, the wilderness temptation places Jesus at the heart of a *cosmic drama *(of celestial region or of spiritual/abstract dimension) **between the kingdom of God and the forces that oppose Him**. The Gospel presentation is not just personal struggle but **spiritual warfare**; Jesus stands in the breach as the Second Adam, confronting the ancient enemy with the full power of the Spirit. The narrative echoes the Garden of Eden, yet this time obedience wins where Adam and Eve failed. In this framework, the Spirit leads Jesus into direct confrontation because He alone can defeat evil's advance, not by avoiding temptation, but by engaging it and emerging victorious. Theologians such as Greg Boyd and Michael Heiser describe Christ's wilderness test as a declaration of war against the flesh and spiritual darkness. - (Restoration Theology — Restoration Theology, 2025). For believers, understanding testing as cosmic conflict brings gravity to personal spiritual battles. Temptation is not only internal, but marks participation in God's larger purpose against darkness. Winning these battles with the help of the Spirit mirrors Jesus' path and **expands the influence of God's kingdom.**

From the three points of view as Synthesis:

Testing as Multifaceted Divine Strategy

These three frameworks do not compete but weave together into a detailed picture of God's work in moments of testing. Spirit-led trials serve to refine character, prepare for future service, and overcome spiritual opposition—often at the same time. In the wilderness, Jesus' story models the multidimensional strategy of God: temptation's fire makes loyalty to God visible, empowers readiness for ministry, and defeats the schemes of the enemy. For Christ's followers, this synthesis offers comfort that struggles never have a singular purpose. The Spirit's leading does not mean absence but is an active shaping for greater likeness to Christ, deeper trust, and spiritual victory. - (Koffa & Seminary, 2025; Restoration Theology — Restoration Theology, 2025). The path of Jesus through His own wilderness stands as a living invitation to walk with the Spirit—knowing He trains, purifies, and equips, every step of the way.

Summary and Reflection of Chapter 11

Now that we have explored **the Spirit's leading of Jesus into the wilderness** through the lenses of purification, preparation, and cosmic conflict, we can better appreciate how this moment reveals God's complex work in times of struggle. **Rather than seeing trials as setbacks or signs of divine absence**, <u>we recognize them as purposeful encounters where faith is tested and strengthened</u>, <u>ministry readiness is shaped</u>, and <u>spiritual battles are engaged with power</u>. This multifaceted understanding encourages us to approach our own hardships not with fear, but with trust that the Spirit is actively guiding us toward growth and victory. As we move forward, this chapter invites young believers and leaders alike to embrace challenging passages with curiosity and confidence, knowing that within difficulty lies the opportunity to become more like Christ and to participate in God's unfolding story.

Reference List of Chapter 11:

Primary Biblical Reference:

Matthew 4:1 … "***Jesus was led by the Spirit*** *into the wilderness* ***to be tempted by the devil****.* Bible – New International Version.

Other References

Koffa, I. C., & Seminary, B. T. (2025, October 27). *Systematic theology volume II. redone docx*. - researchgate.net

Matthew. (2025). - soniclight.com.

O'Donnell, D. (n.d.). *Matthew | Commentary | Douglas Sean O'Donnell | TGCBC*. – thegospelcoalition.org

Restoration Theology — Restoration Theology. (2025). *Restoration Theology*. - restorationtheology.org

Chapter 12:

Rare Case of...

'A MOMENT's VISION in Time'

Satan Showing Jesus "All the World's Kingdoms" in an Instant

<u>Luke 4:5</u> "*And **the devil**, taking him up into a high mountain, **shewed unto him all the kingdoms** of the world **in a moment of time**". **According to; (the Bible) – King James Version.**

*A Moment; Present and Beyond

"When **Satan showed** Jesus 'all the kingdoms of the world <u>in a moment of time</u>,' <u>he revealed more than just lands and borders</u>. This rare vision compressed vast power and influence into <u>a single instant beyond ordinary human experience</u>. Such a glimpse challenges us to consider what it means for authority to be displayed so completely and swiftly, ***outside the limits of space and time**. It invites reflection on the forces shaping societies, beliefs, and destinies, and on how temptation operates when every form of worldly control is presented at once. Exploring this unusual moment helps uncover layers of **meaning that have intrigued scholars and believers** alike—raising questions about spiritual power, the nature of true authority, and the profound choices faced by one called to lead without succumbing to the allure of easy dominion."

José E. Espinoza

Vision Mechanics and Symbolism (structure, imagery, and setting)

The vision in Luke 4:5, where <u>Satan displays</u> *"all the kingdoms of the world in a moment of time,"* <u>stands apart from regular human perception</u>. By using the phrase *"in a moment of time,"* Luke signals an **experience that defies the gradual and limited grasp of the senses**. 'There is no suggestion of a physical journey', nor 'any unfolding panorama for Jesus to watch piece by piece'; **the world's kingdoms appear together, compressed into a single, undivided instant**. <u>This total immediacy marks the event as supernatural</u>, cutting past earthly restraints. The reality of what Jesus sees takes shape **outside the standard flow of time**, providing a revelation all at once, rather than in increments. When writers of the New Testament described moments of divine revelation or prophetic vision, they often pointed to suddenness or simultaneous insight, and here that pattern heightens the sense that Jesus is facing something no ordinary mind could bear. The temptation's force depends upon this full and comprehensive disclosure. In everyday life, laws of physics, geography, and time order what can be seen or known. The instant vision ignores these boundaries, offering a panorama that would take years, or a lifetime, to encounter naturally. Temptation becomes heavier when every possible kind of power stands before a person at once.

This complete, compressed revelation draws the focus inward, past the mechanics of sight, toward the meaning of kingdoms themselves. **"All the kingdoms"** here does <u>more than gather a list of nations or display boundaries on a map</u>. In ancient thought, kingdoms included more than territory—they pointed to **authority, social order, philosophy, wealth, and spiritual sway**. When Satan shows Jesus the kingdoms, he shows not just <u>Rome with its armies and law</u>, but <u>Greece and its schools</u>, <u>temples</u>, and <u>systems of knowledge</u>; <u>Egypt's wisdom and trade</u>; <u>Eastern influences that shaped roads</u>, <u>markets</u>, <u>and mythologies</u>. **Each kingdom contains its cultural structures**, <u>values, and ways people pursue power or meaning</u>. The phrase in Luke's gospel signals that Jesus confronts the total scope of human achievement and the diverse ways authority works in the world. Every realm that shapes daily life and destiny—governments, economic systems, schools, even religious institutions—lies spread before Him. What Satan holds out, then, is not a small plot of land or passing title, but an invitation to control how societies order themselves, who rules, and what values stand at the center. **This makes the temptation one of global, even cosmic, reach**. It is not only about external dominance, but also about influencing the beliefs, hopes, and destiny of every people group and culture.

Satan's position in this story is not just as an outside tempter whispering in the ear; <u>he appears as one who can open hidden realities</u>.

In biblical tradition, angels and demons had access to realms and knowledge that lay beyond human reach. Satan offers a vision that only a spiritual being could grant. He serves, for this moment, as a supernatural mediator, revealing more than can be gathered through experience. This role suggests a hierarchy in the spiritual realm: some beings possess a measure of authority and insight, even though that power remains checked by God. **The vision demonstrates** that evil, while real, cannot operate freely or without restraint. The story raises questions—how much does evil know, or see, or control? **How real is the offer Satan makes**? Still, the text shows a being who can make a reality visible but cannot make it his own or guarantee it to others. This sharper understanding of Satan's role helps frame the entire confrontation as one where power, knowledge, and mediation are on display, not merely suggestion or surface temptation. - (*The Great Controversy between Christ and Satan*, 2025). The enemy and opposer **(satan) is both powerful and limited**, both a revealer of what tempts and a frustrated imitator of the divine. Yet we must have very clear, that (satan) **is not** almighty as our Celestial Father God and Supreme King is.

Interpretive Readings and Theological Implication (literal, metaphorical, psychological perspectives and the doctrinal stake)

Three main interpretive frameworks shape how readers and scholars approach the meaning of Satan's vision in **Luke 4:5**: literal, metaphorical, and psychological. Each helps unravel unique layers of the passage, highlighting distinct aspects of Jesus' encounter (**in a moment of time**) with the "kingdoms of the world" and what it reveals about spiritual warfare, human experience, and the reality of God's rule.

POSSIBILITY OF INTERPRETATION 1:

Literal Interpretation

The **literal interpretation treats the vision as a real**, supernatural event. In this view, Jesus is shown the actual kingdoms and empires of the earth, not just as abstract symbols but as visible realities made present by supernatural means. Evangelical commentaries often describe this as an "apocalyptic unveiling"—something similar to the visions in Daniel 7 where symbolic beasts stand for world empires but are seen with extraordinary clarity and presence. - (*Columbia Theological Seminary*, 2022). "**Satan has temporary authority**" in this perspective refers to the biblical teaching that <u>the devil possesses a measure of influence</u> over earthly institutions—sometimes called the "prince of this world" (**see John 12:31**). Commentator Darrell Bock describes it as Satan "actually putting the kingdoms on offer, **making (apparently) a genuine proposal to Jesus** <u>to rule the world apart from the Father's ways</u>." Here, Jesus faces the real temptation of claiming power that Satan can, for a time, bestow. The instantaneous nature of the vision is explained by Jesus being supernaturally enabled to see across time and space. Satan's role as presenter is understood as literal—he mediates the vision and genuinely offers authority "if you will fall down and worship me." In this framework, Jesus' response is seen as a firm rejection of a real, material offer, establishing his refusal to gain the world at the price of true worship.

POSSIBILITY OF INTERPRETATION 2:

Metaphorical Interpretation

The **metaphorical interpretation** reads the passage as a teaching about the **<u>spiritual and moral seduction of power rather than a</u>**

record of physical geography. <u>Here, the "kingdoms of the world"</u> <u>symbolize the allure of influence, glory, success, and recognition</u> <u>offered by the world's systems</u>—what John calls *"the lust of the eyes and the pride of life"* (**1 John 2:16**). Scholars who favor this approach point out that apocalyptic visions in Scripture use dramatic images to make deeper points about allegiance and temptation. "The vision comes packed with the symbolism of dominion and desire," writes N.T. Wright, who notes that "the real battle is not for territory or thrones but for the loyalty of the heart." In this reading, Jesus' temptation is about choosing to pursue God's kingdom through self-sacrifice and faithfulness rather than through shortcuts to power or spectacle. - (*Columbia Theological Seminary*, 2022). The ethical struggle becomes the main focus: would Jesus pursue the world's empty glory, or would he choose "worship the Lord your God and serve him only"? **Satan's role is that of the deceiver**, <u>presenting</u> <u>distorted choices framed as attractive opportunities</u>. The speed of the vision highlights how quickly and powerfully temptation can grip the human imagination, making the case for vigilance in spiritual warfare. **Jesus' answer stands as a model for moral discernment**, <u>refusing</u> <u>to accept power without obedience to God</u>.

José E. Espinoza

POSSIBILITY OF INTERPRETATION 3:

Psychological Interpretation

The **psychological interpretation** <u>examines the scene as an exploration of Jesus' inner struggles</u>—his hopes, calculations, fears, and self-understanding brought into sharp relief and reality. The kingdoms shown might reflect Jesus' psychological wrestling with; **what kind of Messiah he would be**. Would he seize the world's admiration or walk the hard road toward the cross? Evangelical scholar Craig Evans has written how this passage "reveals the full humanity of Jesus, whose mind and heart were touched by real options and desires, yet who chose unswerving loyalty to God's plan." **Psychological interpreters do not deny the reality of spiritual warfare**. Rather, <u>they stress that the battle takes place not just in cosmic realms but within the inner life</u>. Satan's function here could be understood as prompting, taunting, and stirring up these deep questions in Jesus, so the vision's "instantly" quality refers to how thoughts and temptations can flash vividly through the mind even though no real time passes outside. Jesus' response—quoting Scripture and aligning his will to the Father—becomes a victory of heart as well as external obedience. **This makes him relatable**, <u>fully</u>

human in the depths of his experience while never ceding ground to evil.

Combined Approach and Theological Implication of Divine Sovereignty

Each approach helps visualizing the dramatic moment: **literal interpreters** imagine Jesus staring onto a supernatural panorama; **metaphorical scholars** think of him reckoning with the dazzling promises of worldly achievement; **psychological readers** picture him fighting the lonely battle of integrity in his innermost thoughts. In each, the fundamental point remains the same: **Jesus refuses Satan's offer** because he is not drawn in by temporary power or shallow authority.

Divine sovereignty anchors all these perspectives. This theological term refers to God's supreme authority and control over every kingdom—visible or invisible, real or imagined. Whether the scene is interpreted as supernatural vision, symbolic test, or internal trial, every reading affirms that God's rule outshines all other claims to power. - (Patterson, 2016). **Jesus' rejection of Satan is not just personal discipline**; it enacts the victory of God's reign over all false alternatives. The kingdoms may flash before the eyes, but the throne of God endures. **This moment becomes a turning point in the messianic journey**, where the path leads away from cheap power and toward the cross—the true display of God's kingship.

José E. Espinoza

Summary and Reflection of Chapter 12

Understanding **the vision where Satan reveals all the kingdoms of the world to Jesus in a moment of time,** invites us to see beyond a simple story of temptation; it challenges us to grasp the full scope of spiritual authority, human ambition, and divine sovereignty in one compelling moment. Whether we view this scene as a **literal unveiling**, a **metaphor for moral choice**, or **a glimpse into Jesus' inner struggle**, each perspective deepens our appreciation of how power is presented and rejected. Now that we have explored its symbolism, setting, and interpretations, we can better engage with the ongoing spiritual battle between worldly allure and faithful obedience. **This insight prepares us to recognize** similar temptations in our own lives and encourages us to hold fast to the higher calling exemplified by Jesus—a commitment to serve God's true kingdom rather than fleeting earthly glory.

Reference List for Chapter 12:

Primary Biblical Reference:

Luke 4:5 "*And **the devil**, taking him up into an high mountain, **shewed unto him all the kingdoms** of the world **in a moment of time**".* **According to; (the Bible) – King James Version.**

Other References:

Columbia Theological Seminary. (2022, December 19). Columbia Theological Seminary. - ctsnet.edu

Patterson, D. L. (2016). *The Kingdom of God as a Framework for Evangelical Biblical Hermeneutics*. - sbts.edu. - hdl.handle.net

The Great Controversy Between Christ and Satan. (2025). -gutenberg.org

Chapter 13:

Rare Case of ...

A 'Tentative OFFER':...

In Exchange to Worship the Impostor

Matthew 4:8-9

8) Again, the devil took him to a very high mountain and showed him *all the kingdoms of the world and their splendor. 9)* **"All this I will** **give you**,*"* *he said, "***if you will bow down and worship me**.*"* **(Bible)** – NIV. And other versions

Satan's Proposal of Power in Exchange for Worship

Power and influence <u>have long captured human imagination</u>, often seen <u>as the ultimate goals that confer status, control, and success</u>. Yet, beneath the surface of these ambitions lies a profound question about where true authority originates and **what cost is attached to its pursuit**. Throughout history, many have faced choices between integrity and expedience, faithfulness and compromise, <u>especially when power comes with a demand for loyalty that challenges</u> **fundamental principles** <u>and core beliefs</u>.

This chapter explores **a <u>rare and striking episode</u>** from the Gospel of Matthew, where Jesus faces <u>a temptation unlike any other</u>—a direct offer of all the world's kingdoms **in exchange for worshiping the one who opposes God**. It examines the nature of this offer, its spiritual and ethical implications, and the weight of Jesus' response. We will consider various ways this moment has been understood, including what it reveals about the source of legitimate power, the identity and mission of Jesus as Messiah, and how it shapes Christian ideas about worship, authority, and spiritual struggle. Through this study, readers are invited to reflect on the **challenges** of loyalty and integrity in the <u>face of tempting shortcuts</u> within faith and life.

José E. Espinoza

Nature and Implications of Satan's Offer

All the kingdoms of the world stood before Jesus in a sweeping, visionary panorama—a promise of ultimate influence, unchecked political reach, and dazzling glory. Satan's offer on the high mountain, as recorded in **Matthew 4:8–9**, pulled on the strings of human longing for power, but moved far beyond the temptation to possess or to rule. At its heart, this moment acted as a test of pure allegiance. **When Satan asked for worship in exchange for world dominion**, <u>he demanded the surrender of Jesus' devotion from God to himself</u>. For a first-century Jewish audience, the gravity of this request would have been impossible to miss. Subjecting all peoples—Roman, Judean, and every nation in between—to one authority would have meant grasping the might and status held by the emperors, priests, and kings who shaped the age. The phrase *"all the kingdoms and their splendor"* evoked not just political rule but the sway over armies, laws, economies, and even cultures. Yet **the offer carried a shadow**: <u>worshiping Satan</u> would mean breaking the shema, the burning core of Jewish monotheism, and **shattering the first commandment** <u>to have no other gods</u>. - (Guzik, 2015). Such a move would not just dethrone God from Jesus' heart but unravel the very mission for which he came. The ethical weight becomes clear—no act of "doing good" through worldly rule can justify idolatry, and so the dilemma pivots around the source and the price of power itself.

Looking more closely at the authority behind Satan's proposition, questions rise about who truly holds sway over earthly systems. An intriguing enigma; That Satan can even propose such a trade indicates he claims a form of power over the political and social order of the world. - (Guzik, 2015; *What Was the Meaning and Purpose of Jesus' Temptations?*, n.d.). **This doesn't mean he is the ultimate owner**, but rather a usurper allowed temporary (illegal) rule, as many biblical passages frame him as *"the god of this age"* (**2 Corinthians 4:4**). Since Adam's failure in Genesis, **the human race, stewarded to reign over the earth**, handed spiritual authority to the adversary by turning away from God. - (Guzik, 2015). **Satan's readiness to "give" kingdoms** hints at his influence over governments and rulers— echoing later biblical warnings that powers and authorities can be spiritually corrupted. In the scene on the mountain, he stands as a power broker, tossing the prize of earthly leadership toward Jesus if only he'll acknowledge Satan's claim to worship. Behind these lines lurks another challenge: Is Jesus truly the King, or must he receive legitimacy from the one who opposes God? Accepting the offer would mean conceding that the route to messianic kingship runs through compromise and not divine appointment.

The messianic stakes in this encounter reach beyond personal ambition or momentary influence. At issue is whether **Jesus will seize an immediate**, visible kingdom rooted in politics, or choose a path marked by suffering and spiritual transformation. **A direct rule**, with all earthly splendor, promised conquest over Rome and Jerusalem alike—imagine a Messiah ushering in peace through military victory, popular acclaim, and social control. Yet such a kingdom, dazzling as it appeared, remained hollow compared to the spiritual reign Jesus later inaugurated—one defined by healing, forgiveness, and resurrection. The cross lay at the horizon as a test: **Would Jesus take the shortcut**, skipping over sacrifice and embracing comfort, or accept the long journey with its pain and ultimate vindication? Jesus' refusal in this pivotal episode draws a bright line between the temporary shine of worldly kingdoms and the enduring reality of God's reign. - (*What Was the Meaning and Purpose of Jesus' Temptations?*, n.d.). **The rarity of this temptation stands out**. Rulers and revolutionaries have often traded away ideals for expedient wins, but here, the price is so clear—**immediate gain at the cost of betraying God's love**.

Beneath the politics and theology, the scene wrestles with a deep ethical and spiritual dilemma. Worship offered in exchange for power is not just a subtle moral test but a frontal assault on integrity and trust. **The temptation crystallizes how easy it is**, when offered **a shortcut** to influence, **to sacrifice principle** for advantage. In the real world, shortcuts might look like bending values to rise in a job, abandoning honesty to win favor, or shifting loyalty to gain acceptance. **What makes this moment so rare** is its directness—there is no hidden cost, **only the stark choice to betray God** for something dazzling but fleeting. By sending Satan away, Jesus models the power of resisting temptation through Scripture and steadfast love for God above all returns. - (Guzik, 2015; *What Was the Meaning and Purpose of Jesus' Temptations?*, n.d.). Choosing integrity shuts out easy paths and keeps desire in check.

Standing at this crossroads with Jesus invites many questions about the nature of his victory and the layers of meaning in his refusal. In later traditions, theologians have viewed his response as a standard for resisting evil, a statement about the kind of Messiah he would be, and a call to live out undivided loyalty to God. This opens a wide field for exploring how the church and faith communities understand the cost, authority, and the shape of **true kingdom of God** here on earth.

Interpretations of Jesus' Response and Implications

Evangelical **interpretations of Jesus' response** to Satan's temptation, <u>reveal several interconnected layers of meaning that have shaped Christian understanding and practice</u> for centuries. A close reading of this event uncovers not just an isolated act of moral courage, but a crossroads of ethics, theology, and mission.

POSSIBILITY OF INTERPRETATION 1:

Jesus; Resisting Idolatry

The first possibility of interpretation centers on **Jesus as the one who boldly resists idolatry**. Satan's demand—fall down and worship me—articulates a temptation that strikes at the heart of monotheistic faith. To bow down, even momentarily, would be to surrender the loyalty that belongs only to God. Jesus replies with unwavering commitment, essentially echoing Deuteronomy: *"Worship the Lord your God and serve him only"* (**Matthew 4:10**), framing his allegiance within the scriptural command that underpins all of Israel's covenant faithfulness. - (Schmutzer, 2008). In evangelical commentary, this stance is held up as the decisive model for believers: the refusal to trade fidelity in God for any worldly gain, regardless of the cost. One commentator notes, "The true test of worship is not the presence of options, but the refusal to consider any rival, however attractive." - (*Matthew 4 9 Meaning, Cross Ref, Commentary. Bible Versions; KJV NIV ESV NLT... and other versions*, 2025). Here, Jesus' resistance to idolatry is set against the backdrop of the failures of Israel in the wilderness and the first Adam. Unlike these forerunners, Jesus withstands when tested where others fell, affirming the principle that identifying with God means rejecting all spiritual shortcuts, even those promising instant reward. For Christians, this ethical precedent becomes a touchstone—giving up total devotion is precisely where spiritual defeat begins.

POSSIBILITY OF INTERPRETATION 2:

Assertion of Divine Sovereignty

A second evangelical perspective highlights **the assertion of divine sovereignty**. <u>In this reading, Jesus' refusal directly challenges the legitimacy of Satan's offer.</u> **Authority over the kingdoms of the world rightly belongs to the Messiah**, <u>but it is granted by God</u>, not seized through a bargain with evil. **Satan, presenting himself as a power broker**, <u>can only counterfeit what truly belongs to the Creator</u>. Evangelical scholars often argue, "Jesus refuses because he does not require Satan's patronage. His kingdom is a gift, not a transaction." - (*Matthew 4 9 Meaning, Cross Ref, Commentary KJV NIV ESV NLT*, 2025). Jesus' kingly identity is recognized in his baptism and reaffirmed in his temptation, mapping onto the triadic (or Trinitarian) relationship of Father, Son, and Holy Spirit. - (Schmutzer, 2008). **By rejecting Satan's shortcut**, <u>Jesus demonstrates that true power comes through submission to God's will</u> rather than manipulation or compromise. The event, then, becomes not a contest of wills but a **demonstration that all authority belongs to God**, and <u>only a Messiah rooted in divine legitimacy can rule</u>. The implication for Christian life is profound: genuine authority is received through obedience, not grasped through worldly means.

POSSIBILITY OF INTERPRETATION 3:

Implications for Jesus' Mission

The third possibility of interpretation focuses on the **missional implications of Jesus' decision**. Many scholars argue that this was a defining moment, setting the trajectory for everything that followed.

<u>By refusing the allure of temporal kingdoms secured through compromise</u>, Jesus declares that his mission will not be accomplished through dominance or politics but through suffering, service, and redemption. The so-called "shortcut" would have nullified the cross by substituting immediate power for lasting salvation. As one evangelical author puts it, "Salvation does not come at the price of worshiping evil, but by bearing the cost of obedience." - (*Matthew 4 9 Meaning, Cross Ref, Commentary KJV NIV ESV NLT*, 2025). Jesus' path would now be one of costly faithfulness, his kingdom characterized by humility rather than conquest. This vision reshaped expectations for the Messiah: not a political liberator, but a savior who rescued through self-giving love. - (Schmutzer, 2008). For believers, the call to mission echoes with a similar demand for integrity and spiritual priorities.

POSSIBILITY OF INTERPRETATION 4:

Symbolic Representation of Spiritual Warfare

A fourth, complementary possibility of interpretation, explores this exchange as a **symbolic representation of spiritual warfare**. In the dramatic confrontation, the cosmic battle lines are drawn—good versus evil, truth against deception, and heaven countering the rebellion of Satan. Evangelical interpretation often sees this as <u>a microcosm of spiritual struggles every believer faces</u>. "Jesus' triumph over temptation sets the pattern for all who would battle for righteousness." - (*Matthew 4 9 Meaning, Cross Ref, Commentary KJV NIV ESV NLT*, 2025). The dialogue itself has the feel of a legal dispute or controversy, as seen in other biblical genres. - (Schmutzer, 2008), **dramatizing that ultimate victory comes** <u>when divine truth stands unyielding in the face of false promises</u>. The spiritual authority Jesus demonstrates empowers his followers to do the same.

Each perspective brings out a different color in this rare moment—resisting idolatry points to ethical loyalty, divine sovereignty affirms Jesus' rightful kingship, missional clarity shapes the purpose of his ministry, and the motif of spiritual warfare captures the ongoing challenge for faith. **The kingdom Jesus reveals is not built by shortcuts** or conquest <u>but is defined by the demands of worship, authority grounded in divine purpose, and spiritual integrity</u>.

Summary and Reflection of Chapter 13

Now that we have examined the powerful and rare temptation in **Matthew 4:8–9**, we understand how Jesus' refusal reveals key truths about loyalty, authority, mission, and spiritual battle. This moment challenges us to consider where true power comes from and **what it costs to remain faithful**. Recognizing that worldly gain offered by evil is always tied to compromise helps us see why Jesus' choice matters—not only for his identity as Messiah but for how we live out our faith today. As we move forward, **this insight invites deeper reflection** on resisting shortcuts that threaten our integrity, embracing a mission shaped by sacrifice and service, and standing firm in spiritual struggles with confidence rooted in God's sovereignty. **By holding fast to the example Jesus** sets here, we can better navigate our own temptations and participate faithfully in the kingdom that the true King came to establish.

Reference List for Chapter 13:

Primary Biblical Reference:

<u>**Matthew 4:8-9**</u>
*8) Again, the devil took him to a very high mountain and showed him <u>all the kingdoms of the world and their splendor</u>. 9) "<u>**All this I will give you**</u>," he said, "<u>**if you will bow down and worship me.**</u>"* (Bible) – NIV. And other versions …

Other References

Guzik, D. (2015, December 9). *Matthew Chapter 4.* - enduringword.com

Matthew 4 9 meaning, Cross Ref, commentary KJV NIV ESV NLT. (2025). - jcgm.org

Schmutzer, A. J. (2008). *Jesus' Temptation: A Reflection on Matthew's Use of Old Testament Theology and Imagery.* - academia.edu

What was the meaning and purpose of Jesus' temptations? (n.d.). - gotquestions.org

Chapter 14:

Rare Case of...

"It Is WRITTEN"

Scripture as Weapon, Shield, and Principle Against Temptation

Matt. 4:3-10. & Luke 4:3-11. According to; the Bible – (NIV, - ESV, - KJV, NAS, AMP… and other versions.)

*Phrase <u>to Resist</u> (with) and (against Satan)

The *Written <u>Word of God</u>

What happens when words become more than just letters on a page—when they turn into powerful weapons against doubt, fear, and temptation? How can ancient **Scripture** guide someone facing intense spiritual challenges today? These questions touch on a profound mystery: how does **God's Word** <u>hold authority</u> and strength in real moments of struggle? Many people wonder why certain phrases from the Bible can bring peace or courage when life feels overwhelming. Others ask how those same words can protect and even advance us in battles that seem invisible but deeply personal.

As we consider these questions, we begin to see a pattern revealed through one of the most well-known yet deeply challenging stories in the New Testament—the wilderness temptations faced by Jesus. What makes his use of Scripture so striking is not just the words themselves, but the way he calls upon them again and again with confidence, as if citing an unshakable truth that shapes both thought and action. This repeated declaration, **"It is written,"** invites readers to reflect on how Scripture functions not only as guidance but also as a source of power and identity.

By exploring this pattern, we gain insight into how **Scripture** <u>can be more than a collection of ideas</u>; it becomes a **living resource** <u>that equips and transforms</u>. The story encourages believers to look beyond surface-level familiarity with biblical texts and to engage with them intentionally, allowing their meaning **to guide choices**, **resist temptation**, and **shape daily life**. This chapter invites you into a deeper understanding of **how God's Word** <u>serves as law, defense, and guiding principle—a foundation for navigating both urgent trials and everyday decisions.</u>

Jesus' Use of Scripture in Temptation (Context, Strategy, and Lived Integration)

The wilderness narratives in **<u>Matthew 4:3–10 and Luke 4:3–11</u>** place Jesus in direct confrontation with the tempter. Each challenge he faces is sharp and calculated, testing his identity, loyalty, and trust in God. When the devil urges him to turn stones into bread, leap from the temple's pinnacle, or bow in exchange for worldly kingdoms, Jesus never responds with vague gestures or mystical phrases. Instead, he reaches for **specific passages** in Deuteronomy, <u>quoting with purpose</u>: "***It is written***, '*<u>Man shall not live by bread alone</u>,*'" "***You shall worship the Lord your God and him only shall you serve***," and "*<u>You shall not put the Lord your God to the test</u>*." These responses show that his use of Scripture is not haphazard but demonstrates **precise interpretive** judgment.

Jesus chooses each text because it meets the challenge directly. Faced with the temptation to satisfy hunger by supernatural means, he recalls Israel's wilderness experience and the lesson that true life depends on every word from God, not on material provision alone. When taunted to prove his divinity by a spectacular display, **Jesus refuses the demand for proof**, <u>citing a commandment against testing God</u>. Offered all the kingdoms in exchange for worship, **He reaffirms God's exclusive claim to allegiance**. In each case, the cited Scripture addresses the heart of the temptation, not just the surface need or offer. **Jesus models** <u>what it looks like to bring scriptural truth to bear</u> where temptation strikes, using the written word as a tool both of insight and resistance. - (*Interpretation of the Bible in the Church:* n.d.). This reveals that faithful interpretation is not a rote exercise, but requires discernment: **knowing the text**, <u>reading its intent</u>, and matching it to the demands of the present moment.

The repeated formula, **"It is written,"** <u>signals more than just familiarity with the sacred writings</u>. Each time Jesus pronounces these words, he is making **a clear statement about authority of the written word of God**. <u>He chooses to place himself under the binding rule of God's revelation</u>, submitting to the Creator's directives rather than bowing to the compelling presentations of the adversary. Where the tempter's words aim to twist Scripture's meaning or take it out of context, <u>Jesus returns again and again to what God has declared</u>.

Through this posture, Jesus displays a pattern for navigating ethical dilemmas by seeking divine guidance before acting, rather than relying on instinct or the persuasive voice of the tempter. - (2025). This approach showcases how 'The **Holy Scriptures' (Word of God in The Bible),** <u>serves as the law that governs spiritual life</u>, carrying greater weight than impulse, opportunity, or even basic needs like hunger or safety.

Scripture's dual role becomes clear in this exchange: it serves both as <u>shield and sword</u>. When confronted by accusations, manipulations, or outright lies, Jesus' quotations do more than block or deflect—they actively counter and defeat the attacks. Quoting, *"Man shall not live by bread alone,"* he blocks the lure of self-gratification but also <u>asserts trust in God's provision</u>. By refusing to test God, Jesus cancels the legitimacy of the devil's challenge and asserts integrity in relationship with God. In each of these replies, the dynamic power of God's Word becomes evident as it functions as an active participant in the spiritual conflict rather than just a passive background resource. - (*Interpretation of the Bible in the Church:* n.d.; 2025). The Word used in this way does not simply provide a safe barrier; it carries the fight to the enemy, exposing falsehood, illuminating the right path, and overruling the tempter's proposals.

Jesus' method reaches beyond clever retorts. He inhabits the truths he quotes, aligning his behavior with the principles he declares. As he wrestles with real hunger, the offer of acclaim, and the possibility of shortcutting God's plan, he lets the words of Scripture shape his resolve and actions. **This integration of belief and practice** demonstrates that **the authority of God's Word** is not meant for intellectual assent alone, but for transformation of character. His obedience to the text confirms that the Word is not neutral or abstract—it is living, meant to dwell within and surface in times of testing. Jesus signals that the defense against temptation is found not only in knowing Scripture but in letting it inhabit the heart and guide the will.

Readers are drawn into this pattern not as distant observers but as active participants. The way Jesus wields Scripture in the wilderness points to the resources available for every believer engaged in daily struggles of faith and obedience. It calls for careful attention to what is written, gratitude for the defense Scripture supplies, and a willingness to let the Word reshape life from within. This sets a pattern for deeper reflection on how interpretation and application intertwine and lays the groundwork for exploring the practical frameworks and habits that help anchor faith in God's written promises.

Three Interpretations of Scriptural Authority in Spiritual Battle (Armor, Pattern, and Principle)

When thinking about how Jesus responded to temptation with the words, **"It is written,"** three ways of understanding Scripture's authority come into focus for evangelical Christians. Each one sheds light on a different aspect of the <u>believer's relationship with the Bible</u>, showing how **the words of God** serve as <u>spiritual armor</u>, a model for <u>resisting evil</u>, and a set of <u>guiding principles</u> shaping everyday life.

POSSIBILITY OF INTERPRETATION 1:

Scripture as Spiritual Armor

Ephesians 6 describes the Christian's call to *"put on the full armor of God,"* with the ***"sword of the Spirit, which is <u>the word of God"</u>*** <u>as both offense and defense</u>. Through this lens, Scripture becomes active protection against spiritual attack. Jesus turns to Deuteronomy when Satan tempts him, not with clever arguments but with direct, **memorized truth**. These Scriptural responses aren't improvised.

They come from <u>deep knowledge and internalization of God's Word</u>, demonstrating what John Stott describes as "the defensive armory on which our faith and hope depend." The effect is clear: as the enemy confronts Jesus, every temptation meets the sharp, steady rebuke of *"It is written."*

Memorizing and meditating on Scripture <u>strengthens spiritual resilience</u> just as a soldier learns to use and trust his gear. Daily engagement with the Bible—morning devotions, small group studies, or Scripture memory—builds a ready store of truth. Think of a young believer, facing anxiety before a big decision, drawing on **Philippians 4:6-7** learned weeks earlier. That verse becomes a shield, blocking panic and inviting peace. Billy Graham once said, "The Bible is the only thing that can combat the devil." Each time a believer arms themselves with Scripture, they participate in the victory Jesus displayed in the desert.

POSSIBILITY OF INTERPRETATION 2:

Scripture as a Pattern for Resisting Evil

Jesus' use of "<u>It is written</u>" <u>also stands out as a **repeatable model**—a strategy that commands imitation.</u> This understanding rests on the truth that spiritual resistance isn't automatic. General religious activity or vague good intentions don't stop temptation; rather, it's the targeted application of God's Word that breaks the power of lies. Dallas Willard called this the "intentional effort of mind and will" to bring truth into direct contest with falsehood.

The process is straightforward: recognize the form of temptation, recall Scriptural truth that addresses it, and answer temptation with that truth. For example, when struggling with jealousy, quoting **1 Corinthians 13:4** ("Love does not envy") moves the heart toward God's character. When confronted with peer pressure, recalling **Galatians 1:10** ("Am I now trying to win the approval of men, or of God?") gives courage. This is not passive hope for escape, but deliberate preparation. Through Bible study and discipleship, young adults learn how to identify their weak spots and collect "ready verses." John Piper writes, "Every time you resist a temptation by trusting a promise of God, you are living out the same victory Jesus did." Temptation is battled by faith meeting the right Scripture at the right moment.

POSSIBILITY OF INTERPRETATION 3:

Scripture as Principle for Christian Living

The authority of "It is written" reaches beyond moments of crisis. For evangelical Christians, **Scripture** provides the standard not only for fighting spiritual battles, but for shaping life every day. This approach sees **the Bible** as the highest norm for choices, ethics, attitudes, and sense of identity. **Psalm 119:105** describes God's Word as "a lamp to my feet and a light to my path"—ongoing, gentle guidance through every season.

In friendships, the teaching of Proverbs on kindness and honesty lays the groundwork for real relationships. At work, **Colossians 3:23** ("Whatever you do, work at it with all your heart…") shapes effort and integrity. Even in leisure, the call to honor God or love others steers decisions. As J.I. Packer puts it, "Scripture shapes all that we are and do, not only what we believe." Bible study leaders can help others see how **"It is written"** isn't only a rule in emergencies, but a foundation for living as a Christ-follower every day, within the Kingdom of God here on earth.

The Complementary Function of the Three

These three understandings intertwine in a believer's life, working together more than alone. **In moments of temptation**, a Christian may find protection in a memorized passage, <u>resist evil by actively speaking truth</u>, and reassure themselves that God's standard for living is both clear and good. For example, a student facing pressure to cheat uses Scripture as armor (remembering, "It is written… do not steal"), follows Jesus' pattern by naming the wrong out loud, and appeals to the larger principle that God's truth defines behavior no matter who is watching.

As these frameworks are woven together—**defense and offense, example, and guideline**—the Bible's authority becomes richer and more practical. The believer who views Scripture through all three lenses, finds deeper strength and joy both in moments of trial and in the patterns of ordinary life, learning to trust God's Word as living and active for every challenge and decision.

Summary and Reflection of Chapter 14

Now that we understand **how Jesus used <u>Scripture</u>** in the wilderness—<u>as a powerful authority</u>, <u>a strategic tool against temptation</u>, and <u>a guiding light for daily life</u>—we can begin to see **the Bible** not just as an ancient text but as <u>a living resource for our own challenges</u>. Embracing this approach invites us to engage deeply with **God's Word**, learning to recognize its voice in moments of struggle and decision. **By following Jesus' example**, <u>we can prepare ourselves through study and reflection</u>, **equipping our minds and hearts** to respond wisely when tested. This chapter encourages us to move beyond simply knowing Scripture to letting it shape how we live, resist wrong, and trust God's promises, laying a foundation for stronger faith and clearer understanding in both personal journeys and group conversations.

Reference List of Chapter 14:

Primary Biblical References:

Rare 'Phrase to Resist' (with) and (against Satan) "It is Written" (as a Biblical principle and/or Holy Scriptures) Mentioned in **Matt. 4:3-10**. & **Luke 4:3-11**. According to; the Bible – (NIV, - ESV, - KJV, NAS, AMP… and others.)

Other References:

(2025). - reformation21.org

Interpretation of the Bible in the Church: (n.d.). - catholic-resources.org

PART 5:

Rare Cases of ...

The *OPPOSSER

A Deceiver to *Rob, - A *Lethal Appealing, - A Fatal *Destruction

Chapter 15:

Rare Case of…

The Tempter's TACTIC:

Satan Strategy; as a 'Primary Method' …(?)

<u>Luke 4:9-11</u> and <u>Matthew 4:5-7</u> According to; the Bible – (NIV, ESV, KJV, NAS, AMP… and Other Versions)

José E. Espinoza

'Incorrect Use' of the Holy Scriptures

Have you ever wondered how **something meant to protect and guide us** could be turned into a tool for deception? What happens when words that offer comfort become twisted to create confusion or temptation instead? These questions challenge us to think carefully about **the power and use of Scripture in our lives**. How can the same sacred texts that inspire faith also be misused to mislead or manipulate? This chapter invites you to explore **a rare and striking example** from the New Testament where such a reversal takes place. As we examine this moment, we will **uncover important lessons about understanding Scripture deeply**, guarding against false interpretations, and developing spiritual wisdom that helps us stand firm when faced with subtle challenges.

Analysis of Satan's Misuse of Scripture (Luke 4:9–11; Matthew 4:5–7)

The clash in the wilderness between Jesus and Satan is more than a dramatic showdown; **it demonstrates just how dangerous it is when Scripture is twisted and taken out of contex**t. The Gospels of Luke and Matthew describe <u>Satan's **attempt to challenge Jesus** by quoting from Psalm 91</u>: "He will command his angels concerning you, to guard you," and, "On their hands they will bear you up, lest you strike your foot against a stone." What Satan presents is clever because it sounds spiritual, but it is **manipulation**—a **tactic** that still appears in various forms today. - (*Matthew 4 Commentary | Precept Austin*, 2024). Satan leaves out the crucial context: Psalm 91 describes the security of <u>those who dwell in the shelter of the Most High</u>, **<u>not those</u> who test that security through <u>reckless acts</u>**.

One of the **tempter's <u>first tools</u> is <u>selective quotation</u>**. <u>This means isolating a verse or phrase from its original context to create an artificial meaning—something also known as proof-texting</u>. **Proof-texting** <u>takes words meant for one purpose and repackages them for another</u>. In this story, Satan snatches a few lines from a psalm—removing them from the relationship, trust, and obedience called for throughout Scripture—and presents them as blank checks for miraculous intervention. The problem is that by removing words from their wider narrative, the tempter guts them of the humility, patience, and dependence that shape their true meaning. In contemporary terms, proof-texting can look like someone cherry-picking verses to justify an argument or behavior, without wrestling honestly with the full scope of the Bible's teaching—like using "**judge not**" to silence all moral evaluation, or wielding "**I can do all things**" to bless any goal, no matter how unrelated to God's will. - (*Matthew 4 Commentary | Precept Austin*, 2024; Daneshmand, 2021). The result is a misleading framework that pressures Jesus to validate His identity through a spectacle rather than quiet trust.

The **second tactic runs even deeper**: testing **Jesus' identity and obedience**. At first glance, Satan's challenge is about whether Jesus really is the Son of God. Under the surface, the real contest involves trust and patience. Is Jesus willing to wait and let His Father reveal His identity and power in the fullness of time, or will He seize an opportunity to prove it on His own terms? Satan's test tries to push Jesus away from humility and dependence on God and toward presumption—demanding that God act in spectacular ways to justify belief. While the psalm (91) promises angelic protection, **it never tells someone to throw themselves into danger just to prove God's faithfulness**. These same temptations play out now when people misuse God's promises as excuses for risky decisions or self-promotion, twisting words meant for comfort into tools for self-centered behavior. - (*Matthew 4 Commentary | Precept Austin*, 2024). Faith doesn't demand God jump through hoops for us; it waits, trusts, and stays grounded in relationship.

Scripture itself becomes a double-edged sword in this encounter. **The fact that Satan can, and does**, quote from the Psalms should give every reader reason to pause. The power of God's Word lies both in its truth and in the heart that hears it. **Intellectual knowledge of verses is not the same as spiritual discernment**. Without careful attention to context, humility, and the **Holy Spirit's guidance**, even the most sacred texts can be misapplied or weaponized. That's why manipulation of Scripture remains a threat not only in the first century wilderness but in today's pulpits, social media feeds, and personal lives. - (Daneshmand, 2021). This raises an urgent challenge: spiritual battles aren't confined to obvious temptations like anger or pride; they also unfold in realms of doctrine, teaching, and interpretation.

Jesus responds by drawing from Deuteronomy, returning each twisted half-truth with the full counsel of God. He refuses to turn His relationship with the Father into a show for public approval or self-assurance. Instead of responding to Satan's dare, He quotes, **"You shall not put thc Lord your God to the test,"** reminding all who read these words that obeying God never involves forcing His hand or making demands. Jesus demonstrates that knowing Scripture means more than memorizing verses—it requires deep understanding and humility. - (*Matthew 4 Commentary | Precept Austin*, 2024). Where Satan's version isolates and manipulates, **Jesus applies Scripture correctly**: in its original context, centered on faithfulness, trust, and obedience.

In our world, **distorted use of the Bible still appears in many shapes**: <u>a leader twisting verses to gain influence</u>, a viral post quoting scripture out of context, or someone using a snippet of biblical language to justify a questionable relationship or decision. **The danger** is clear—misused Scripture breeds confusion and can even snare well-meaning followers. **Staying safe** <u>means learning the tools to sift truth from error</u>, so that faith grows not only in knowledge but also in wisdom, discernment, and genuine connection with God. These are the tools this chapter invites you to seek as you encounter both truth and temptation.

Three Approaches to Discern and Counter Misapplied Scripture

POSSIBILITY OF INTERPRETATION 1:

Contextual Reading

Looking closely at the context of any Scripture passage is the first and most reliable way to see past misleading interpretations. **Contextual reading** means starting with the **full passage**, not just the verse someone quotes. **It includes looking at the verses before and after**, paying attention to the audience for whom the words were first spoken or written, and asking what was happening in their world at the time. Not all parts of the Bible use the same type of writing—poetry, history, law, prophecy, or letters—so recognizing genre helps set limits on the text's meaning. **Authorial purpose is another key**: What was the writer's goal, and how would the first readers have understood it? Consider **Jeremiah 29:11**, used often to promise personal prosperity: *"For I know the plans I have for you… plans to prosper you and not to harm you."* Isolated from context, it seems like a guarantee of trouble-free success for individuals. Reading just a few verses before and after, readers see the promise was given to Jewish exiles in

Babylon, reassuring them about God's long-term intentions for their community despite difficulty. - (Okafor, 2025). This method also helps prevent superficial readings by rooting interpretation in background study—understanding language, culture, and the writer's intention clarifies what the text meant then and what it can mean now. - (Brian, 2016). When people read Bible passages **in context**, they are less likely to twist or misuse them to support personal agendas or to argue a point out of step with the passage's true intent.

POSSIBILITY OF INTERPRETATION 2:

Spiritual Discernment

Spiritual discernment forms the second half of a wise approach to Scripture. Where contextual reading builds understanding, discernment invites the Holy Spirit to reveal layers of meaning that may not be clear through study alone. **Prayer** and openness allow believers to sense warning signs when an interpretation "doesn't sit right," even if it sounds correct on the surface. **The Holy Spirit's guidance** shows when motives behind certain teachings begin to drift, or when a verse is twisted in subtle ways. Bringing prayer and spiritual attention into Bible reading shifts the mindset from just gaining knowledge to seeking relationship and transformation. For example, someone might encounter a teaching that uses Scripture to justify unforgiveness against others. Reading the passage intellectually might highlight certain rules, but prayerful discernment could bring unease—a sense that the overall message of Jesus calls for forgiveness and mercy, not bitterness. Sometimes, intellect gives facts, but spiritual discernment prompts readers to ask, "Does this use of the Bible match the full character of Christ?". - (Brian, 2016; Okafor, 2025). By pausing, asking God for clarity, and listening for inner conviction or peace, believers <u>invite the Holy Spirit to help align interpretation with God's heart</u>. This sensitivity is not opposed to intellectual study; they work together.

POSSIBILITY OF INTERPRETATION 3:

Community Accountability

Accountability within a trusted community <u>builds on the first two methods</u>. Whether through a Bible study group, mentor, or local church, shared discussion brings out perspectives and insights one person might miss. No one reads the Bible free from personal bias, background, or emotional influence. **Talking through a passage with others** spotlights where individual interpretation drifts or where experience might be blinding someone to what the passage really means. For instance, a member of a group may share an opinion about a difficult teaching—others might gently challenge or support that view, encouraging a fuller look at the text and sometimes offering historical or cultural background that had been overlooked. These relationships foster humility, correction, and safety, guarding against error and individual pride. People learn to welcome correction as an act of love, and as a way to read Scripture faithfully rather than simply to get their own way. - (Okafor, 2025). In another example, **a mentor could help someone** recognize when they are reading wishes or fears into a passage.

Combining these 3 Approaches for Robust Defense

Each of these methods—contextual reading, spiritual discernment, community accountability—offer solid, practical defense, yet they are strongest when used together. **<u>Contextual reading</u>** gives the **intellectual** tools for weighing <u>interpretations</u>. **<u>Spiritual discernment</u>** adds the "gut check" and real-time guidance of the Holy Spirit. **<u>Community accountability</u>** provides <u>shared wisdom</u>, empathy, and correction, protecting against the errors and blind spots that come from isolated reading. His response to Satan (Jesus correct responses with the Scriptures), embodied this three-fold approach—a sharp mind, a tuned heart, and a faithful relationship to God's community and heritage. - (Brian, 2016). **This triple layering forms a powerful**

safeguard <u>against manipulation or misuse of God's Word</u>. In the wilderness, **Jesus knew the Scriptures by heart**, <u>understood their context</u>, <u>stayed connected to the Father</u> (showing spiritual discernment), and drew on the faithful tradition of His people.

Self-Help Exercise: "Triple-Check Bible Application"

Purpose: This exercise builds skill and confidence in safe, faithful Bible interpretation by guiding readers through the three methods together. It prepares believers to spot misuse, hear God's voice, and welcome community wisdom.

Steps:

- Choose a passage or verse you've recently heard or want to explore further.
- Start with Contextual Reading:
- Read at least ten verses before and after your chosen passage.
- Ask: Who wrote this? Who was the first audience? What was happening at that time? What type of writing is this?
- Write down the main message in your own words based on this bigger picture.
- Engage Spiritual Discernment:

- **Pause and pray**: "<u>Holy Spirit, help me</u> see the truth here. Warn me if I'm misunderstanding or missing something."
- Notice your gut reactions—are you uneasy, resistant, or at peace? Why?
- Ask yourself: Does this understanding fit with the message and character of Jesus?
- Find Community Accountability:
- Share what you've learned and your insights with a trusted friend, Bible study group, or mentor.
- Invite feedback: "Does this make sense to you? Do you see it differently? What do you notice in these verses?"
- Take notes on any corrections or new perspectives offered.
- Reflect and Apply:
- What changed about your interpretation after these steps?
- How might you apply the passage to your life based on this process?

Applying the previous methods/steps will help you greatly with your reading and Bible interpretation. "Each time you practice, you will grow in wisdom, awareness, and maturity in handling God's Word". - (Brian, 2016; Okafor, 2025). So, let this portion of this book be a blessed spiritual tool for you, throughout your journey entering The Kingdom of God.

Summary and Reflection of Chapter 15

Now that we understand **how Satan twisted Scripture** <u>to tempt Jesus,</u> we are better equipped to recognize and resist similar misuses in our own lives. This chapter has shown us the **importance of reading Bible verses with care**—<u>looking beyond isolated phrases</u> **to grasp their full meaning** <u>within context</u>—and seeking the guidance of the Holy Spirit alongside the wisdom found in community. By combining <u>careful study</u>, **spiritual discernment**, and honest conversation, we can protect ourselves from being led astray by distorted interpretations and grow stronger in faith. As we move forward, let us approach Scripture not just as words to memorize, but as a living guide that calls us to trust, humility, and obedience, helping us stand firm amid the challenges of today's spiritual battles.

Reference List of Chapter 15:

Primary Biblical Reference:

Luke 4:9-11 and **Matthew 4:5-7** According to; the Bible – (NIV, ESV, KJV, NAS, AMP… and Other Versions)

Other References:

Brian. (2016). *Towards a global theology: Theological method and contextualisation.* - verbumetecclesia.org

Daneshmand, J. L. (2021). *The Elusive Jesus of Luke-Acts in Its Ancient Mediterranean Literary Context.* - academia.edu

Matthew 4 Commentary | Precept Austin. (2024). - preceptaustin.org

Okafor, C. (2025, August 21). *Understanding Different Biblical Interpretations: A Guide for Believers - GospelLight Creations.* - gospellightcreations.com

Chapter 16:

Rare Case of…

The *OPPOSER as

'*Tempter'

Duration, Intention, and Spiritual Reasons (to Discover)

Matthew 4:10. and **Luke 4: 13** – (Bible) – (Various Version)

José E. Espinoza

The Tempter & The Temptations

What does it really mean **to be tested**? Or to be tempted by (***satan**) the ***opposer**? How long can endurance stretch before faith begins to waver or grow stronger? And **what happens inside a person when facing spiritual opposition** that seems unrelenting? These questions reach into the heart of one of the most intense moments recorded in Scripture—the forty days Jesus spent in the wilderness, **confronted by satan's temptation**. This period is much more than a historical event; it offers a window into understanding the timeline and intention behind spiritual testing and the ***tempter**, as well as its deeper consequences. As we examine the nuances of the opponent in this experience, we uncover how prolonged trials shape character, **reveal true reliance on God's Word**, and prepare for the challenges ahead. What can this ancient encounter of **Jesus resisting the adversary**, teach us about enduring hardship, preparing for ministry, and maintaining vigilance over time? Exploring **this rare case of the opposer** along with these themes will invite fresh insight into **why testing matters** and how it functions within a believer's journey.

Timeline, Duration, Intent, Proof, and Defeat

Extended periods of testing carry a spiritual weight that presses far beyond the circumstance itself. When Jesus faced the opposer or tempter, during forty days of temptation in the wilderness, the pain and deprivation were not simply means of discomfort. These hardships laid the foundation for core lessons about spiritual growth, faith, and ministry. Looking into these lessons can help readers extract the same strength to confront the opposer and for their own journey of faith.

Growth Through Adversity

James 1:2-4 establishes that <u>facing trials brings endurance</u> and ultimately leads to spiritual maturity, **forming a person's character**. As the passage says, *"Let perseverance finish its work so that you may be mature and complete, not lacking anything."* Jesus experienced hunger, loneliness, and relentless temptation, enduring the full force of adversity, while refusing to surrender to the temptations presented by the devil. John Stott captures this truth, writing, "For every Christian, adversity can be like a refiner's fire or like a purgatory. The important thing is to know that God walks with us in the fire." Steadfastness in trouble transforms and strengthens, not because the pain disappears but because perseverance births resilience.

The desert was not just an empty landscape. Every hunger pang and whisper from the tempter gave Jesus a deeper opportunity to depend on God rather than on self-preservation. It is when resistance is most costly—when one's physical and emotional reserves are low—that authentic strength is born. In these moments, comfort is not the standard for spiritual talent. Instead, as Dietrich Bonhoeffer reflected, "Only he who believes is obedient; and only he who is obedient believes." Perseverance in adversity molds a person far more effectively than uninterrupted seasons of peace. - (*The Temptation of Christ - Luke 4:1-13*, 2023; Guzik, 2015).

When believers face elongated suffering—a chronic illness, repeated disappointments, or persistent spiritual dryness—they are refined by the furnace of hardship. The ashes of shattered expectations often become the ground for new growth, enabling a faith that is sturdy, deep-rooted, and patient. The desert story of <u>Jesus confronting the tempter</u> makes clear that spiritual maturity is forged not primarily in moments of ease but in the hard-earned victory of holding on through adversity.

Testing of Faith as Ministry Foundation

Testing **often reveals the substance of faith**, <u>exposing both strengths and vulnerabilities</u>. In the wilderness, Jesus did not debate with the devil using human logic or opinion. Instead, he wielded Scripture, quoting passages such as, "It is written, 'Man shall not live by bread alone, but by every word that proceeds from the mouth of God.'" With each retort, **faith in God's promises became his shield**. Charles Spurgeon put it plainly: "**The Word of God is the sword of the Spirit**; <u>never use your own sword</u>." For Jesus, tested faith was not merely private but became the foundation—solid and proven—that empowered every later ministry moment.

Evangelical commentators highlight that the repeated use of Scripture during temptation was not accidental, but demonstrated total reliance on God as opposed to self-dependence. - (*The Temptation of Christ - Luke 4:1-13*, 2023; Guzik, 2015). Real faith emerges when pressure rises, when resources run out, and when the enemy's voice gets loud. Surviving the trial is not just about gritting one's teeth; it's about clinging to God's Word as the only sure anchor. D.A. Carson observes, "Authentication comes only after the test. Tested faith is reliable, for both present conviction and future battle."

This tested reliability (in answering the opposer with written word of God) is exactly what Jesus would need as crowds gathered and opposition mounted in his public ministry. Victory in the desert battle prepared him to heal, to confront religious hypocrisy, and to shoulder the loneliness of Gethsemane. Testing uncovers a faith worth sharing and defending, forming the backbone of every effective ministry.

Preparation for Ministry

The period of Jesus confronting to satan and the wilderness isolation, was not just defensive; it was a **time of divine preparation**. <u>Solitude with the Father allowed for undistracted communion</u>, helping Jesus **distinguish the voice of God** from the lies of his adversary. **Testing (or temptations from de opposer) was an essential part of the preparation**, as it exposed the tactics of evil while sharpening spiritual focus. Richard Foster notes, "Solitude is the furnace of transformation." Intense, personal reflection—combined with the battle against temptation—acted as training for the confrontation, healing, and teaching that lay ahead.

Preparation in the desert had a dual nature: **confrontation with opposition**, and disciplined withdrawal. Both facets were necessary. Withdrawal fostered clear discernment and renewed purpose, while confrontation toughened spiritual resolve. Spiritual disciplines—

prayer, fasting, meditating on Scripture—are still foundational tools used for equipping believers for their calling. - (*The Temptation of Christ - Luke 4:1-13*, 2023; Guzik, 2015). Out of the silence meditation in the Spirit, resistance to the adversary with the word of God and struggle to suffer with endurance, emerged clarity—Jesus saw with absolute focus what his calling demanded.

Ongoing Spiritual Reality & The Opposer as Tempter

Luke 4:13 tells us that **the devil departed** from Jesus (temporarily) "until an opportune time." This single line communicates that spiritual warfare is not an isolated event but a repeating cycle. Battles won in one season do not erase the reality of future attacks from the opposer. Yet, Jesus' example gives every believer hope. **God arms us with the Word** and strengthens us by his Spirit. Temptations and spiritual struggles will return, but **the methods for victory remain constant**. Corrie Ten Boom's reassurance, "There is no pit so deep that God's love is not deeper still," becomes a lens for understanding spiritual vigilance. Rather than a source of dread, the ongoing nature of spiritual testing allows growth, dependence on God, and the regular opportunity for victory that shapes genuine spiritual resilience. Readers are reminded that repeated challenges from the tempter are normal and that, modeled after Jesus' experience, each trial becomes a new arena for faith to grow.

Interpretive Lessons, Preparation for Ministry, and Ongoing Opposition

POSSIBILITY OF INTERPRETATION 1:

Growth Through Adversity: Strengthening Character and Resolve

Jesus' forty days in the wilderness confronting the opposer, deliver a blueprint for **how adversity shapes spiritual maturity**. His struggle was not a momentary event but an ongoing test, stretching across days when He faced physical hunger, isolation, and relentless temptation. This span gave room for the slow work of spiritual character. While Satan's approach aimed at exploiting human weakness, Jesus endured every wave, letting the hardship become the soil for deeper strength. In **James 1:2–4**, believers receive the same encouragement: *"Consider it pure joy, my brothers and sisters, whenever you face trials of many kinds, because you know that the testing of your faith produces perseverance. Let perseverance finish its work, so that you may be mature and complete, not lacking anything."* This passage frames adversity not as a detour but as the main path to spiritual completeness.

During His fast, Jesus felt real human frailty; His body surely called out for relief. Yet, **in this weakness**, a mysterious strength rose up, showing the pattern Paul names in **2 Corinthians 12:10**: *"...For when I am weak, then I am strong."* As participants in one study testified, adversity often became the catalyst for spiritual growth, reframing hardship from problem to possibility and making space for transformation. - (Manning et al., 2019). Charles Spurgeon captured this truth plainly: "The gem cannot be polished without friction, nor man perfected without trials." **The process of enduring/resisting the tempter or the temptation**, rather than escaping, leads to faith that is both gentle and tough. For those facing life's hardest moments—illness, loss, or uncertainty—Jesus stands as a model of one whose inner life was refined through suffering, not in spite of it. Every pressure point became an invitation to let **faith** deepen, grow resilient, and emerge proven.

POSSIBILITY OF INTERPRETATION 2:

Testing of Faith as a Foundation for Ministry

The wilderness experience reveals another lesson: **spiritual trials do not merely weigh down faith—they reveal its genuineness**. Each temptation presented by opposer, pressed Jesus not just to show His power but to rest on God's Word. When Satan challenged Him, Jesus answered not with clever arguments but by **quoting Scripture**. This pattern underscores the place of God's Word as **both shield and sword** in all spiritual conflict. When Jesus declared, *"Man shall not live on bread alone, but on every word that comes from the mouth of God,"* He demonstrated that faith isn't just a feeling; it's grounded in reliable promises. - (Matthew 4:4).

Jesus' responses marked Him as someone whose faith had real roots—tested, stretched, and proven trustworthy. This kind of faith stands ready for bigger challenges. After the confrontation with the devil in the wilderness, Jesus entered His public ministry where **He faced opposition from religious leaders, crowds pressing in, and dark spiritual forces**, but His foundation was sure. Evangelical teachers often emphasize that time spent learning, memorizing, and applying Scripture prepares people to recognize falsehood and hold steady in tough seasons. - (University, 2025). As one preacher put it, "A Bible that's falling apart usually belongs to someone who isn't." The hard test before ministry became the anchor for everything that followed.

POSSIBILITY OF INTERPRETATION 3:

Preparation for Ministry: Equipping Through Spiritual Discipline

Jesus' time in the wilderness confronting satan's temptations, shows how preparation often requires **intentional challenge**. Instead of viewing this as survival mode, He used every moment <u>for spiritual discipline</u>. Solitude was paired with confrontation: Jesus withdrew physically to meet the Father but stayed alert for Satan's schemes. These dual elements mirror the way growth happens not only through external conflict but also quiet listening for God's guidance. The isolation stripped away distractions, sharpening Jesus' sense of mission and commitment to the Father's will.

This pattern offers a guide for anyone called to serve. <u>Effective ministry never grows from untested enthusiasm</u>; it needs seasons set aside for focused spiritual tuning. As one participant in a study described, time alone, journaling, and self-reflection helped them recognize both God's presence and patterns of temptation. - (Manning et al., 2019). **Contemplative prayer**, **silent attention**, and **Scripture reading** become central tools for discernment. - (University, 2025). **Ministry readiness comes not just from facing public tests**, but from times in the "wilderness," learning to listen, endure, and prepare. Without such times, even good intentions can break under pressure.

The Reality of (*satan) Continued Spiritual *Opposition

The **closing note of Jesus' temptation**, *"when the *devil (*Satan or the *opposer) had finished all this *tempting, **he left him** until an opportune time."* - (**Luke 4:13**), warns that **victory** is often partial, **not total**. **Spiritual battle is not one-and-done** but ongoing. Jesus' resistance forced the tempter to retreat, but not to concede defeat forever. This detail underscores the realistic nature of spiritual warfare for believers. **Temptation and challenge will return**, sometimes in new forms or at unexpected moments.

This reality keeps disciples alert. The armor of God, described in **Ephesians 6:11**, is not for a single battle but for a lifetime of resistance. Paul says, *"Put on the full armor of God so that you can take your stand against the *__devil__'s schemes."* Knowing struggle will revisit us means building habits of vigilance—Scripture, prayer, and spiritual community that can hold ground, when the tempter with his temptations finds another "**opportune time**."

Jesus' wilderness resistance becomes a living example for every believer's journey. **Rather than promising escape from spiritual struggle**, it assures that through sustained discipline, scriptural grounding, and honest dependence on God, we can stand, recover, and press forward each time the test returns. - (Manning et al., 2019; University, 2025).

Summary and Reflection of Chapter 16

Now that we have explored the rare case of **the opposer** as **tempter** through Jesus' forty days of wilderness testing, its timeline, purpose, and spiritual significance, we can better understand how trials shape faith and prepare for ministry. **This chapter shows** that <u>enduring hardship builds strength and maturity</u>, revealing the true nature of our trust in God. Jesus' reliance on Scripture during temptation (facing ***satan**), teaches us to anchor ourselves in God's Word when facing challenges, while His time of solitude highlights the importance of quiet preparation alongside spiritual battle. Recognizing de reality that **spiritual struggles will continue** reminds us <u>to stay vigilant, equipped with prayer and Scripture to stand firm</u>. With these insights, young believers and leaders alike can approach their own journey with confidence, knowing that perseverance through testing is not only expected but essential for growth, service, and lasting faith.

Reference List of Chapter 16:

Primary Biblical Reference:

Matthew 4:10. and **Luke 4: 13** According to; Bible – (Amplified Holy Bible Version)

Other References:

Guzik, D. (2015, December 9). *Matthew Chapter 4.* - enduringword.com

Manning, L., Ferris, M., Narvaez Rosario, C., Prues, M., & Bouchard, L. (2019). *Spiritual resilience: Understanding the protection and promotion of well-being in the later life.* Journal of Religion, Spirituality & Aging. - doi.org

The Temptation Of Christ - Luke 4:1-13. (2023). Saint Ignatius Community. - st-ignatius.net.

University, C. (2025). *Embracing Life Challenges: Keeping the Faith During Difficult Times | CCU Online.* - ccu.edu.

PART 6:

RARITY OF...

A KINGDOM; DIVINE & EARTHLY

Fusion of Heavens & Earth

Chapter 17:

Rare Case of...

"The WILD BEASTS"

Literal Creatures or Symbolic Forces? (In the Wilderness/Temptation of Jesus):

Mark 1:13 ..."Was with <u>the Wild Beasts</u>,"... - According to; the Bible – (New *King James Version)*.

José E. Espinoza

Terrestrial/Spiritual; Conflict or Coalition

When we picture Jesus in the wilderness, we imagine silence stretched wide, broken only by the rustle of unseen creatures, (and/or possibly visible for Him). But what did it mean when **Mark said**, *"and was with the **wild beasts**"*? Were these **animals/**(entities); **literal** dangers lurking in the desert, **symbols** of deeper spiritual battles, or something else entirely? **This question has puzzled readers and teachers** alike, inviting us to pause and wonder about the layers hidden in just a few words. The story's wilderness is no simple backdrop—it challenges us to look closely at who Jesus was and what his time alone in the desert facing temptation, reveals about the struggle between threat, peace, and power."

Contextual Background and Theological Significance

The brief line in **Mark 1:13**—**_"He was with the wild beasts"_**—has sparked a whole range of interpretations, each one opening up a new way of looking at **Jesus' wilderness experience**. Instead of choosing between them, it helps to see how these views can sit together, each shining a different light on what might seem like a small detail.

Some have always taken the <u>wild beasts</u> quite literally. <u>To them, these animals were real</u>, actual creatures living in the Judean wilderness. This landscape was known for its lions, jackals, foxes, wolves, bears, snakes, and scorpions—hardly a safe place for anyone spending forty days alone. **Reading the text this way**, <u>Jesus' encounter with wild beasts draws attention to his physical vulnerability</u>. The dangers were not just spiritual or emotional; they were sharp-clawed, fast-moving, and very real. Fasting for forty days would have left Jesus physically weakened, surrounded by constant threats. His risk of hunger and vulnerability to any attack fits with the larger remarking <u>emphasis on Jesus' full humanity</u>—the Son of God does not escape ordinary dangers and pain, but lives them out in full. When Mark says Jesus <u>*"was with the wild beasts,"*</u> it plants the reader squarely in the heart of that stark, **risky reality**, with no attempt to soften it. - (Mark 1:13; Squires, 2021). Facing down wild animals in the desert deepens the seriousness of his testing. The wildness and isolation make the story more than spiritual symbolism; they underline that Jesus' struggle was embodied, risky, and would have been felt with every sense. This reading ties into the larger Gospel message: Jesus' solidarity with the human experience includes being exposed to threat, hunger, and fear.

Beyond the literal, the **symbolic interpretation** draws on <u>how wild beasts function throughout the Bible</u>. In prophetic literature, wild animals show up again and again <u>as avatars of chaos, judgment, and evil</u>. Isaiah describes the wilderness as the "haunt of jackals" where evil powers roam. - (**Isaiah 13:21**). Jeremiah uses images of wild creatures to express the total spiritual desolation that comes when God's order breaks down. - (**Jeremiah 50:39**). **Readers seeing Mark's wild beasts** this way, <u>recognize a whole tradition of animals standing in for spiritual danger</u>, rather than physical threat alone. In this light, the presence of beasts in the wilderness with Jesus hints at the **spiritual battle** underneath the surface—temptations are not just internal struggles, but <u>confrontations with the evil</u> **powers that resist God's rule**. The wilderness itself was known as a place where evil spirits and demons lurked. - (*The Haunting of Jesus: Reading Mark through the Gothic Mode – Journal for Interdisciplinary Biblical Studies*, 2022). Jesus' "testing by Satan" comes with the company of **wild beasts**, <u>underlining the sense that all the powers of chaos and destruction are arrayed against him</u>. Readers who take this path see the beasts as more than a narrative detail; **they are symbols of the spiritual enemies** Jesus faces when he stands between God's will and Satan's opposition.

Taking things in a different direction, there is a view that focuses on the peace between Jesus and the wild animals. Rather than picturing a hostile encounter, some readers see a hint of companionship, or at least mutual acceptance. This idea grows out of how the Greek construction in Mark points toward a peaceful relationship, one that echoes God's promise for a healed creation. **Isaiah 11:6-9** famously describes the future peaceable kingdom, where *"the wolf shall dwell with the lamb...and a little child shall lead them."* Jesus' presence among the beasts, without harm befalling him, prefigures this age of harmony. - (Squires, 2021). Instead of defense or fear, the scene suggests authority—animals who might normally be dangerous do not attack. **Some call Jesus the new Adam**, living out the harmony with creation lost since Eden. Others see a sign of **the Messiah, who brings shalom to all of God's world**, not just to people but to the land, water, and wild creatures. **The appearance of angels serving Jesus** alongside docile beasts further amplifies this reading: here is a Lord who commands both the natural and supernatural realm.

Rather than forcing a choice between these, the fourth and most layered reading brings all three lenses together. According to many scholars, **Mark's Gospel** is full of symbolic textures and historical memories at once. The forty days in the wilderness was absolutely full of real dangers, including wild animals. At the same time, the animals would have called up for Mark's audience a host of biblical images of chaos, evil, and demonic powers. On top of this, the companionship or presence of **beasts** hints at restoration—Jesus does not come only to survive the wilderness, but to redeem it. **Mark's language** allows all of these meanings to exist together: Jesus is literally exposed to wild animals, fights a spiritual battle with Satan, and displays a peace that hints at God's promised future. - (Squires, 2021; *The Haunting of Jesus: Reading Mark through the Gothic Mode – Journal for Interdisciplinary Biblical Studies*, 2022). This layered interpretation lets us see how the story works on many levels, inviting readers to find both **immediate reality and deep theological promise in a single phrase**. The wild beasts may be a minor detail in terms of space, but their presence in the Gospel narrative invites deeper reflection on the complexity and depth of Jesus' wilderness ordeal.

Approaches to Interpreting "Wild Beasts" in Mark 1:13

Examining **Mark's phrase** *"he was with the wild beasts"* <u>opens the door to several interpretive paths</u>, each offering its own insights into the text and into the identity of Jesus. Four main approaches shape discussion among scholars, pastors, and students: **literal**, **symbolic**, **authority-over-creation**, and **combined interpretations**. Each draws on Scripture and theology in meaningful ways.

POSSIBILITY OF INTERPRETATION 1:

<u>Literal Interpretation</u>: **Facing Real Danger and Human Vulnerability**

Looking first to the literal approach, some readers see Mark's reference as a <u>straightforward observation</u>. Here, the **"wild beasts"** are found in the Judean wilderness—wolves, jackals, serpents, or leopards, (and other possible naturals animals). Accepting this detail at face value highlights the **real physical danger Jesus endured**. <u>**Mark 1:13**</u> places Jesus in an exposed, isolated setting where threats came not only from spiritual sources, but **from the natural world** as well.

This reading strengthens our grasp of the Incarnation. It affirms that **Jesus' humanity** included the <u>experience of bodily risk and discomfort</u>. He did not enter a symbolic or sanitized wilderness; instead, the challenges He faced were immediate and real. His ability to endure hunger, heat, exposure, and the presence of wild animals underscores His full participation in the human condition, not just in spiritual testing, but also in every form of human vulnerability. - (*BYU Studies*, 2025). By confronting the same dangers as people in His day, Jesus' suffering becomes more accessible and relatable to those who face their own wilderness trials, both great and small.

POSSIBILITY OF INTERPRETATION 2:

<u>Symbolic</u> Interpretation: Spiritual Chaos and Demonic Opposition

Moving from natural threats to spiritual ones, <u>the symbolic interpretation</u> explores biblical use of **"wild beasts"** as <u>figures for evil, chaos, and demonic forces</u>. Prophets often used the imagery of dangerous animals to represent hostile or destructive spiritual realities.

Isaiah 13:21 paints a desolate land filled with wild creatures—a picture of chaos after judgment. **Jeremiah 50:39** speaks of jackals and wild animals as symbols for Babylon's barrenness and spiritual abandonment.

Following this line, some readers find that the "wild beasts" of Mark 1:13 <u>point beyond the literal animals to a deeper spiritual battle</u>. Jesus does not simply struggle against hunger or thirst. His solitude among the beasts mirrors earlier biblical stories where chaos and danger stand for evil's presence. Standing firm, Jesus defeats not only Satan's temptations but also the whole realm symbolized by the threatening beasts. - (Gibson, 2022). The wilderness becomes a battleground for spiritual warfare, echoing how Scripture depicts Satan as a roaring lion seeking to devour. - (1 Peter 5:8).

For listeners and readers, this approach highlights the reality of spiritual struggles. It invites reflection on ways evil, temptation, and chaos still prowl in the wilderness seasons of life.

POSSIBILITY OF INTERPRETATION 3:

Authority-Over-Creation Interpretation: The Peaceable Kingdom Foreshadowed

Another perspective interprets the passage as a statement of Jesus' authority and divine mission. In this view, **"he was with the wild beasts"** shows a miraculous peace and mastery, as dangerous creatures do not harm Him. The image recalls the prophet Isaiah's vision of a restored creation: *"The wolf will dwell with the lamb, the leopard will lie down with the young goat… They will neither harm nor destroy on all my holy mountain."* - (**Isaiah 11:6-9**). In Jesus' wilderness sojourn, peace reigns where violence once ruled.

This reading points to **Jesus as the one who brings the peace of God's kingdom**, beginning the restoration of harmony between humanity and creation. Rather than being attacked or frightened, Jesus' presence tames the wilderness, signaling His power over every realm—spiritual, physical, and cosmic. - (*BYU Studies*, 2025; Gibson, 2022). **The scene** foreshadows His ultimate victory, not only over temptation, but over decay, death, and the disorder introduced by sin.

José E. Espinoza

Combined View: Layers of Meaning in Mark's Wild Beasts

Many Bible study leaders and careful readers recognize that Mark's narrative style encourages multiple layers of meaning. The **literal** and **symbolic** are not mutually exclusive but build on each other. Jesus' presence among literal animals communicates both the raw risk of His mission and His entry into the full scope of human danger, while the symbolic dimension expands the story's reach into the realm of spiritual warfare and the defeat of evil's power.

At the same time, the notion of authority-over-creation overlays both literal and symbolic readings, pointing toward the **renewal and hope embedded in Jesus' ministry**. Mark's mention of the wild beasts, in its simple brevity, suggests a convergence of these truths: the real risk Jesus accepted, the broader battle He fought, and the ultimate victory He began to reveal. - (Gibson, 2022).

Approaching **Mark's detail** about the **wild beasts** through any one of these interpretations invites deeper reflection, but holding all together as a rich tapestry can help young adults and Bible study groups ponder **Jesus' unique identity** as both human and divine, conqueror of chaos, and bringer of peace. Each lens adds dimension to the story, encouraging trust and hope for wilderness journeys today.

Summary and Reflection of Chapter 17

Now that we have explored the different ways to understand Jesus' time "**with the <u>wild beasts</u>**" in the wilderness—<u>literal danger, spiritual battle, peaceful authority</u>, and their combination—we can appreciate how this brief phrase <u>opens a rich window into His identity and mission</u>. Recognizing these layers invites us to see Jesus not only as **fully human**, <u>facing real risks</u>, but <u>also as the one who confronts evil and restores peace to creation</u>. This deeper understanding encourages us to trust Him more in our own difficult times, knowing that His experience in the wilderness holds meaning beyond the surface. As we reflect on these insights, we are better equipped to lead thoughtful discussions, strengthen faith, and find hope when facing our own challenges.

José E. Espinoza

Reference List of Chapter 17:

Primary Biblical Reference

Mark 1:13 …"Was with the Wild Beasts,"… - According to; the Bible – (New *King James Version*). *And other Versions…*

Other References:

BYU Studies. Theology in the Gospel of Mark (2025). - byu.edu

Gibson, J. B. (2022, September 23). *Jesus in the Wilderness: The Purpose of His Wilderness "Temptation"* - academia.edu

Squires, J. T. (2021, February 16). *Forty days, led by the Spirit: Jesus in the wilderness (Mark 1; Lent 1B).* An Informed Faith – johntsquires.com

The Haunting of Jesus: Reading Mark through the Gothic Mode – Journal for Interdisciplinary Biblical Studies. (2022, July 19). - hcommons.org.

Chapter 18:

Rare Case of…

'ANGELS Serving' Jesus

Rescue, Ministry, Metaphor, …or …(?)

<u>Matthew 4:11</u>. According to; the Bible – (New *American Standar*d Bible); "<u>Angels</u> came and began <u>to *serve* Him</u>". And – (NIV); …Angels came… "*<u>to attend</u>* Him" – (NLT); …Angels came… "*<u>took care</u>* of Jesus" – (ESV); …<u>Angels</u> came and were *<u>ministering</u>* to Him.

The Rare case of "Angels Serving Jesus," at the end of the 40 days fasting and 'after' satan finished with all the temptations and left Him alone (in such occasion).

After forty days of fasting and facing relentless temptation in the wilderness, a quiet moment unfolds: **angels arrive to serve Jesus**. This brief scene has intrigued readers for centuries, raising questions about **who these angels were** and what their presence means. How should we understand this encounter—as **a real rescue**, **a sign of encouragement**, or **a deeper symbol**? Different Bible translations and interpretations offer varied perspectives, each adding layers of meaning. By looking closely at the language and exploring these views side by side, we gain fresh ways to think about **divine care** that speak powerfully to anyone navigating trials today.

Scene and <u>Translation Comparison</u>: Setting the Questions and How Words Shape Meaning

Among biblical accounts, **<u>Matthew 4:11</u>** stands out as <u>a moment of profound divine interaction</u>: *"Then the devil left Him; and behold, **<u>angels</u>** came and began to **<u>serve Him</u>**."* Unpacking this verse, readers can approach the **angels' ministry** through three interpretive frameworks—each offering unique insights that work in harmony to reveal the richness of heavenly care for Jesus and how this shapes the spiritual imagination of believers today. - (*Matthew 4:11 - Verse-By-Verse Bible Commentary - StudyLight.org*, 2025).

The **literal angelical assistance interpretation** treats the arrival and <u>ministry of angels as a historical reality</u>. Within this view, angels are seen as true heavenly messengers who provided Jesus with the **physical and spiritual support** He deeply needed after forty days of fasting and wrestling with temptation. The phrase **<u>"ministered (Serving) to Him"</u>** <u>indicates the</u> **angels** <u>(possibly) did more than just appear—they tended, aided, and perhaps even offered sustenance</u>, echoing the care shown to other biblical heroes. - (1 Kings 19:5-8). When Elijah collapsed from exhaustion and despair, an angel brought him food and encouragement, reviving his spirit and body for the tasks ahead. In Daniel's story, angelic protection in the lions' den was a concrete sign of God's intervention, bringing real safety to Daniel as he faced mortal danger. **"Ministering angels"** <u>found throughout the Scriptures consistently</u> act in direct, tangible ways, which lends weight to the expectation that God can and does act in decisive and practical ways during times of crisis. - (Oluwafemi, 2020). Evangelical Christians often emphasize this straightforward reading because it highlights God's willingness to break into history, offering (what we call) supernatural support in response to genuine need.

Moving to a **symbolic encouragement interpretation**, the angels' presence takes on a strikingly different yet complementary meaning. Rather than focusing primarily on physical aid, this perspective views these angels as symbols of divine affirmation and encouragement at a decisive spiritual moment. **In this reading**, the ministry of the angels represents God's approval of Jesus' faithfulness through temptation and testing. Their attentive presence at the end of the ordeal signals to the reader that God is pleased and actively affirms the resolve and decisive act of His servant. For those enduring spiritual battles today, this imagery functions as a powerful seal—a reassurance that enduring hardship in faith brings not only eventual relief but also God's unspoken '<u>well-done</u>'. Believers facing setbacks or spiritual loneliness may find deep comfort in the notion that angelic ministry symbolizes God's approval, even if their struggles are unseen or unrecognized by others. The "angelical ministry" here could be spiritual and emotional rather than tangible, offering the inner lift so often required during faith-testing seasons. Scripture's symbolic language encourages personal application: when God's approval shines through after a storm, believers receive strength to continue in faithfulness. - (Oluwafemi, 2020). In various theological traditions, such moments of divine encouragement point to God's affirming companionship in the journey through difficulty.

A **metaphorical interpretation** offers another dimension, suggesting the story uses **angels as a literary tool** rather than as a record of supernatural intervention. Here, the narrative's focus shifts from physical events to the enduring truth that God's care transcends visible actions or dramatic rescues. The angels represent an eternal assurance—no matter how isolated or strained, Jesus was never truly alone. Even without direct intervention or obvious miracles, the divine presence sustained Him **in His hour of need**. This approach teaches that God's awareness and compassion are constant, even if they are not always demonstrated in extraordinary manifestations. Many readers find comfort in this, recognizing that their own prayers may not always yield immediate or visible responses, yet God's attentiveness remains sure. By viewing the angels as illustrations of God's unseen care, believers learn to trust in a faithful presence that is not limited to the obvious or sensational. - (*Matthew 4:11 - Verse-By-Verse Bible Commentary - StudyLight.org*, 2025). This metaphorical perspective is supported by evangelical scholars who balance literary interpretation with loyalty to scriptural authority, showing how recognizing literary devices can enhance, not undermine, biblical truth.

Blending these interpretive approaches leads to a fuller, layered understanding. A literal angelic encounter can simultaneously convey symbolic encouragement and function as a metaphor for broader theological realities. For example, when facing a personal crisis, some may experience clear, tangible help, others feel uplifted in spirit, and others rest only in the deep assurance that God remains near. Exploring these frameworks side by side opens up a dynamic, living engagement with the text, inviting young adults to recognize that God provides, affirms, and remains constant, no matter how His ministry appears. - (*Matthew 4:11 - Verse-By-Verse Bible Commentary - StudyLight.org*, 2025; Oluwafemi, 2020). Holding these **possibilities together**, readers might ask: In my own struggles, where do I observe divine help—through friends' support, inner encouragement, or a quiet sense of God's presence? Which interpretation best describes the shape of God's ministry in my life today?

Three Interpretive Readings of Angelic Ministry and Their Coexistence

Angels ministering (serving) to Jesus in Matthew 4:11 has been read and discussed by generations of Christians, each group bringing different interpretive frameworks to the text. Three major approaches remain meaningful for young believers and Bible study leaders today: literal assistance, symbolic encouragement, and metaphorical representation. Each perspective draws on linguistic choices in Bible translation, as well as a wide range of evangelical theological scholarship, to highlight the layers of divine care and support during moments of pressure or trial.

POSSIBILITY OF INTERPRETATION 1:

Literal Assistance: Angels as Divine Caregivers

The **literal angelical assistance interpretation** sees <u>these angels as</u> **actual, supernatural beings** <u>sent by God to render real aid to Jesus</u> after forty days of temptation and fasting in the wilderness. This help could have included both **physical** care—much as angels provided Elijah with food and drink in his own time of weakness (**1 Kings 19:5-8**)—and **spiritual** encouragement, as later described in Gethsemane when an angel strengthens Jesus during his agony (**Luke 22:43**). Evangelical theologians have long argued that such readings align with broader biblical patterns of divine intervention, <u>where God dispatches His messengers to serve and sustain those devoted to Him</u>, not as mere symbols but as active agents participating in God's plan. - (Bonino, 2024). **Hebrews 1:14** describes angels as *"spirits in the divine service, sent to serve for the sake of those who are to inherit salvation,"* supporting this point of view or interpretation. Young believers or newly converted Christians, can find reassurance in the idea that God's care sometimes takes tangible form during our weakest moments, whether that means strength for the soul or needed material provision. This approach encourages those reading **Matthew 4:11** to trust in a God who is near and remains actively involved in the lives of His people.

POSSIBILITY OF INTERPRETATION 2:

Symbolic Encouragement: Angels as Signs of Divine Approval and Comfort

Reading the same passage for its **symbolic** encouragement, interpreters see the appearance of angels after Jesus' victory over Satan not only as an event, but as <u>a visible sign of God's approval</u> and delight in the beloved Son's obedience. Throughout Scripture, God often sends outward confirmations after seasons of testing—rainbows after the flood, doves at Jesus' baptism. Here, **the ministry of angels signals a decisive turning point**: the Father affirms His Son's faithfulness in the face of extreme temptation, just as the angels' hosts at Bethlehem; when they glorified God and proclaimed glorious blessings of Jesus' birth. - (Luke 2:9–14; Bonino, 2024). Some scholars point out that early Christians understood angelic presence in worship as a sign that heaven and earth are joined in moments of deep spiritual importance. **This symbolic reading** brings a message of pastoral hope: when believers pass through difficult tests, **<u>God can send visible or emotional reminders of His care</u>**. Young believers and mature Christians in the faith as well, may recognize such encouragement in answered prayers, kind words from others, or a sudden sense of peace after anxiety. The story reminds readers to look for signs of God's joy and presence, even when circumstances have been draining.

POSSIBILITY OF INTERPRETATION 3:

Metaphor for Divine Care: Angels Represent God's Ongoing Presence and Protection

Those adopting **the metaphorical interpretation** focus on the narrative power of angels to represent God's constant and often unseen presence, without insisting on a physical event. Seeing "angels" this way does not deny the truth of God's care, but highlights the deeper reality behind the story—Jesus was never alone, though human companions were absent. The language here becomes a literary device, chosen to drive home the assurance that God's support remains, even when no rescue seems immediate. - (Bonino, 2024). **This refreshes the way contemporary believers might interpret their own stories**: maybe no angelic figures step into their room, but moments of unexpected comfort, insight, or recovery carry the same message. Evangelical hermeneutics emphasizes that reading Scripture in light of its plain sense still leaves room for layered meaning, provided the context justifies it. - (*A Testimony of Jesus Christ : 2.7 -*

Interpreting Symbols, 2025). For those living through quiet, lonely, or confusing times, the metaphorical approach encourages a search for God's companionship, not only in miraculous events, but also in the small, sustaining graces that arrive quietly.

Interrelated Possibility of Interpretations; Enriching Understanding

Each reading is not an enemy to the others. **Literal**, **symbolic**, and **metaphorical <u>interpretations</u>** <u>often interact</u>, just as different instruments are needed for different notes in a song. When these perspectives come together, they invite richer engagement with Scripture. **One moment can show God's hand as both <u>real and invisible</u>**, practical and profound, tailored to each journey of faith. This opens up questions for reflection: Have you seen God's help in a dramatic or material way? Did you sense approval or gentle encouragement after a test or trial? Where do you notice God's help, even when it does not appear outwardly? Exploring these questions helps young believers and veteran Christians, to move beyond the surface of the text, giving them language and categories to sense God's movement in their own walk—whether through supernatural help, meaningful symbols, or the quiet warmth of a caring presence. - (Bonino, 2024; *A Testimony of Jesus Christ : 2.7 - Interpreting Symbols*, 2025).

Summary and Reflection of Chapter 18

Now that we have explored the **literal**, **symbolic**, and **metaphorical** interpretations of the angels ministering (serving) to Jesus after His wilderness temptation, readers are equipped to engage with this passage in a more meaningful way. Recognizing how these perspectives complement rather than contradict each other, invites young believers and study leaders alike, to appreciate the depth of divine care portrayed—not just as historical fact, but also as powerful encouragement and enduring presence. This layered understanding encourages personal reflection on how **God's support may appear uniquely in each life**, whether through tangible help, reassuring signs, or quiet inner peace. Moving forward, this holistic approach can deepen one's faith journey and inspire thoughtful discussion about how God ministers to us in diverse forms during our own times of trial and growth.

Reference List of Chapter 18

Primary Biblical Reference:

Matthew 4:11. According to; the Bible – (New *American Standar*d **B**ible); "**Angels** came and began **to *serve* Him**". And – (NIV); …**Angels** came… "***to attend*** Him" – (NLT); …**Angels** came… "***took care*** of Jesus" – (ESV); …**Angels** came and were ***ministering*** to Him.

Other References:

A Testimony of Jesus Christ: 2.7 - Interpreting Symbols. (2025). - spiritandtruth.org

Bonino, S.-T. (2024, February 29). *Angels in Christian Theology*. St Andrews Encyclopaedia of Theology. - saet.ac.uk.

Matthew 4:11 - Verse-by-Verse Bible Commentary - StudyLight.org. (2025). - studylight.org

Oluwafemi, E. (2020). *A Comparative Analysis of Christianity and Islam concepts of Angels: the Panacea to Religious Harmony*. - academia.edu.

Conclusion

In drawing this book to a close, we step back and take in the panorama of rare and enigmatic moments described in the four Gospels—encounters that challenge easy assumptions and invite both careful thought and imaginative faith. **The stories or <u>passages explored across these chapters</u> are not the familiar threads most often picked up in Sunday school or casual reading**; instead, they are **<u>the rare cases</u>**—scenes of <u>profound mystery</u>, layered symbolism, and unique intervention <u>that unfold quietly on the margins of the New Testament</u>. By focusing on these passages, we open a path for young believers, Christians with more that few years in the faith, Bible study leaders, educators, and spiritual explorers alike—a path that bridges analytical curiosity with real-life application while avoiding overly technical language, so each reader is welcomed into the journey.

Central to all these **rare Gospel cases** is the idea that God's activity often appears in unexpected ways. They function as invitations—calling us to question what we've assumed about the boundaries between the ordinary and the divine, the natural and the supernatural, the visible and the invisible. Whether the scenario is a baby leaping in the mother's womb at the presence of Jesus, or an angel appearing in a night dream to give instructions, each story asks: Can you see God's hand in **the rare and unusual**, the perplexing, and the easily overlooked?

One of the most **consistent lessons** drawn **from these rare passages** is that God works both before human understanding begins, and beyond where our sense of control ends. **Each possibility of interpretation**—literal miracle, symbol, theological message, or historical explanation—shows that the Gospels are theologically multi-layered, making room for thoughtful debate and shared wonder. For anyone teaching or studying with youth, or adult bible study connect group, it's important to encourage honest exploration here, demonstrating how faith need not shrink from hard questions but can thrive in the middle of them.

Throughout the book, **special attention** is given to the risks and **responsibilities of interpretation** itself. When Satan twists Scripture, weaponizing God's promises for temptation, the stakes for careful reading become clear. Safe engagement with **these ancient texts** requires context awareness, spiritual discernment, and communal accountability. The encouragement offered here is practical: **read widely**, **pray regularly**, and welcome correction and insight from others. This approach doesn't just protect against error, it invites deeper wisdom—a vital resource for young adults and leaders who want faith that matures rather than stagnates.

Another recurring theme is the interplay between **literal experience** and **symbolic meaning**. <u>**The 'wild beasts'**</u> surrounding Jesus at the temptation in Mark's Gospel, the appearance of '<u>**angels Serving or ministering to Jesus'**</u>, and the dazzling '<u>**vision of all the world's kingdoms' compress together**</u> <u>fact and metaphor</u>, present threat and future promise, physical reality and spiritual victory. **The cumulative effect of studying these rare cases** <u>is the cultivation of a faith that welcomes questions</u>, <u>relishes mystery</u>, and <u>remains grounded in the love</u> <u>and character of God revealed in Jesus Christ</u>. For young believers searching for authenticity, for teachers/leaders of group striving to nurture curiosity, and for any seeker of profound biblical truth weary of trite answers, these stories provide fertile ground for transformation. They show that **encountering God** <u>rarely means explaining everything</u> away—instead, it calls us to respond with trust, integrity, and hope **when faced with what is <u>rare</u>, <u>strange</u>, or unresolved**.

Discussion and reflection on these passages do not demand advanced degrees or specialized vocabulary. Instead, what's required is a willingness to listen carefully, think deeply, and walk humbly. **This book encourages readers to share their insights and doubts openly**, to build supportive communities where <u>different</u> <u>**'Possibilities Interpretations'**</u> spark dialogue rather than division, and to model a faith that is robust enough to entertain uncertainty while holding fast to the essentials.

As you leave these pages, the invitation remains: **live with eyes open for the rare cases in your own journey**. Expect God to work in the surprising and the silent, <u>the obvious and the hidden</u>. Trust that He meets you in wildernesses, speaks gently in dreams, offers courage amid temptation, and sends help in both dramatic and quiet forms. Take the lessons learned from these enigmatic passages—God's initiative comes before we ask, His power often appears clothed in weakness, His answers may unsettle before they bring peace—and let them shape how you engage Scripture, community, and your own daily walk.

In summary, exploring the <u>**RARE CASES** in the New Testament</u> does not only expand knowledge; it builds resilience, empathy, curiosity, and confidence. It creates a foundation for a thoughtful, enduring faith—one agile enough for serious study, warm enough for honest questions, and generous enough to embrace differences. May these reflections **equip you to teach**, lead, and learn in ways that honor both the richness of God's Kingdom in this Word and the complexity of the lives it reaches. <u>May your pursuit of understanding continue</u> to bring light, wisdom, and renewal **as 'you discover the extraordinary'** in <u>the stories, passages, or verses in the Bible</u> that at first seem <u>**rare**</u>, but on closer reading, <u>reveal</u> themselves as essential.

The End.

About The Author

José E. Espinoza is a Writer, Instructor, and Christian guide specializing in **Leadership** and personal development for young believers, experienced individuals, and professionals in the walk of faith. He has been a dedicated **Missionary** since his youth; consistently committed to proclaim and sharing **the Evangelical Message of the Kingdom of God.**

Other books from The Author

Available on Amazon:

STRANGE TOPICS BOOK #1

Enigmatic Biblical Phenomena with Possibility of Interpretation: Day One – Before The Flood

Message of Jesus #1

Proclamation of the Kingdom of Heaven on Earth as Primary Objective

NEW LIFE In 3 Priorities of T R I U M P H

Transformation ABC In The Kingdom of God